# PIRATE HOSTAGE

## Faith & a Dog Named Beaux Saved My Life

## CAPTAIN WREN C. THOMAS
### WITH LORI A. VANGILDER-PREUSS

TITLETOWN
PUBLISHING

# PIRATE HOSTAGE

TitleTown Publishing, LLC
P.O. Box 12093 Green Bay, WI 54307-12093
920.737.8051 | titletownpublishing.com
Publisher: Tracy C. Ertl

PUBLISHER'S CATALOGING-IN-PUBLICATION DATA:

Names: Thomas, Wren C., author. | VanGilder-Preuss, Lori A., author.
Title: Pirate hostage : faith & a dog named Beaux saved my life
/ Captain Wren C. Thomas and Lori A. VanGilder-Preuss.
Description: Green Bay, WI : TitleTown Publishing, [2022]
Identifiers: ISBN: 9781955047173
Subjects: LCSH: Thomas, Wren C. | Ship captains--Biography. | Hostages-
-Nigeria--Biography. | Piracy--Nigeria--Personal narratives. | Hijacking of
ships--Nigeria--Personal narratives. | Hostages--Psychological aspects. |
Post-traumatic stress disorder--treatment. | Service dogs--Psychological
aspects. | LCGFT: Pirate captivity narratives. | Autobiographies. |
BISAC: BIOGRAPHY & AUTOBIOGRAPHY / Personal Memoirs. |
BIOGRAPHY & AUTOBIOGRAPHY / Aviation & Nautical.
Classification: LCC: HV6433.786.N6 T56 2022 |
DDC: 363.325/09669--dc23

## ACKNOWLEDGMENTS

Thank you to Rhonda, Sheri, Brenda, Kari, and the rest of my family, who inspired me to write this book. I am in debt to Brenda for the relentless hours she put into her research. Thank you to my Attorney, Brian Beckcom, for finding Beaux at Tackett Service Dogs in Orange, California. I genuinely want to thank Tracy Ertl and Lori VanGilder-Preuss for their tireless help writing and publishing my horror story. It was a long journey, but my account finally came to life. I hope that the Marine Industry will start taking Pirates seriously and that the companies whose men have faced pirates, as I have, will start giving those seamen and their families the help they need. Pirating is a serious business in Nigeria and the rest of the world and needs to be stopped.

A ship in port is safe,
but that's not what ships are built for
JOHN A. SHEDD

1492. As children, we were taught to memorize this year with pride and joy as the year people began living full and imaginative lives on the continent of North America. Actually, people had been living full and imaginative lives on the continent of North America for hundreds of years before that. 1492 was simply the year sea pirates began to rob, cheat, and kill them.

KURT VONNEGUT, *Breakfast of Champions*
US novelist (1922–2007)

# CONTENTS

# WHO IS WHO

**Captain Wren Thomas** – Captain of *C-Retriever*. Called Tommy to his family and called Stone Cold Steve Austin and Mr. Stone by the kidnappers and fellow hostage.

**HiLo\*** – American chief engineer kidnapped with Captain Thomas \*real name edited in the interest of privacy

**Deno Chouest** – Head of the Overseas Division Edison Chouest Offshore, LLC

**Brent Chaisson** – Manager of the West Africa Division

**Albert Falgout** – Manager of Nigeria Division in Nigeria

**Ken Idehan** – Nigerian Manager in Nigeria (Albert's relief same position)

**Ben Sanamo** – Coordinator under Brent

**Warren Sanamo** – Designated person ashore

**Mel Comeaux** – company security officer

**Wayne Johnson** – Warehouse Manager in Onne, Nigeria

**Kenneth (Doc) Bailey** – Warehouse Manager in Onne, Nigeria (Wayne and Kenneth relieve each other)

**Seamar** – Leader of Pirates

**Seaman** – 2nd in command of Pirates

## CHAPTER ONE

# Happy Captain at Sea

### Captain Wren Thomas

Sitting in the wheelhouse, I triple-checked the computer screens for the ship and the radar screens and confirmed that everything was satisfactory on the bridge. Then, I took a moment to grab my coffee and step out to the deck. It was a beautiful day. The vast, deep blue seas were calm, with softly flowing waves, the water glistening in the bright daylight, and the air was incredibly crisp and clean.

Days like today reminded me why I enjoyed being a Captain, sailing my ship, and getting a little wind therapy, just as I do when riding my Harley. In addition, I had a good crew on this trip, which always made the voyage more enjoyable.

When I was finishing high school, a cousin contacted me and urged me to move to Louisiana and work on boats. So naturally, I jumped at that chance. So two days after graduating, I moved to Louisiana and started working for Tidewater Marine.

I learned a lot about being a mariner at Tidewater. All the companies I have worked for with offshore drilling rigs have taught me more about the industry. It did not take long to set the goal of being a ship captain, the best Captain I could be.

I worked, learned, and studied hard. Then, I went to school

and received my Captain's license in 1991. To attain my dream of becoming a Captain meant a lot. It took strength and hard work and was a significant accomplishment.

Finally, I was in charge of my destiny.

From then on, I could travel the world while working for various shipping firms. I remember when I contracted to make deliveries across the Caribbean Sea to Trinidad-Tobago. I can laugh now, but those trips were challenging, with rough seas the entire way. We were constantly battling swells, getting rained on, with bad visibility. But, challenging or not, I loved those trips. I enjoyed the exposure to other cultures and meeting the locals wherever I traveled.

For about a year, I worked in the Indian Ocean. It was always calm weather, smooth seas, and plenty of wind therapy. While there, I had a good crew and clients. As always, I enjoyed the exposure to new cultures and people.

As I sipped my fresh cup of coffee, I looked at my mug, a Christmas gift from Ruby, my stepdaughter, with her picture on it. Then, feeling reflective, I took a moment to consider how fortunate a man I am. I have a good wife, Rhonda, and two strong sons, Blake and Dillon, along with Ruby. In addition, I had a close-knit family, including my Mom, Grandmother, and sisters.

I enjoyed spending time with my family and riding when I was home. I was part of a motorcycle club and prospected for a long year before being a full member. It was a brotherhood like no other.

## CHAPTER TWO

# Lagos, Nigeria

In August 2009, I changed positions and started my command on the M/V Deep Stim, a well-stimulation vessel used for oil fracking contracted to Schlumberger, the world's largest oilfield services company. I was under contract as a 2nd Captain under a good friend and mentor from Pensacola, Florida. This ship was ported in Lagos, Nigeria, at the Gulf of Guinea.

Even though the ship was US flagged, the company hired locals to work as able seamen (ABs) on the boat. Locals performed as cooks, stewards, and engineers or performed deck and wheelhouse duties. ABs were to clean, paint, tie, and untie the vessel in port, unload the ship at the rig, and stand watch on the bridge while underway. ABs were also responsible for keeping security watch 24 hours a day while secured in port. The security watch would be a man sitting on the gangway while in port, writing down visitor's names in their log sheet, along with 2 ABs on the bridge when the ship was underway. In Lagos, Schlumberger had 15 workers onboard the vessel, and working with them was challenging.

There were both Schlumberger and Nigerian managers. We had to follow US Coast Guard regulations and Nigerian rules. Working with four sets of rules and regulations was hard. It was also challenging to get the ABs to understand that they had to follow the US Coast Guard rules and regulations, which are much more strict than the Nigerian rules. Honestly, it was a constant battle.

The Nigerian ABs felt they controlled the vessels in their waters and could do anything they wanted. From handling hazardous material chemicals to food, they wanted to do things the Nigerian way in their waters.

To understand their mentality, you must realize that their waters include the Gulf of Guinea, a significant shipping route vital for global trade. Nigeria is the undisputed economic leader in the area. The challenge comes from the fact that those riches do not trickle down to the residents.

The Gulf of Guinea is also the location of a significant amount of oil and gasoline. The Gulf has 2/3 of Africa's oil production and 4.5% of the world's proven oil reserves. Approximately 30% of American oil imports come from or thru this region[1]. Theft of oil is a significant problem and a big business as the locals recognize the value of the gas and oil and the value of the shipping operations in the area.

The locals are also seeing the depletion of their land from oil spills poisoning the waters, poisoning the seafood, a significant stable in the local diet. In addition, the oil is seeping into the ground, killing native plants and trees. A lot of the local damage can be traced to oil theft by locals who do not observe appropriate safety precautions. They will carry oil in any container possible, gas can, water can, and even plastic bags.

They store the oil in holes in the ground, unaware they contaminate their aquifer. Locals have set up homemade gas refineries up and down the various bights and creeks from the Gulf inland. The fires burn brightly in the air, visible for many miles, along with the thick, black smoke.

The locals are surprised when the ground is saturated in oil,

---

1  https://www.gisreportsonline.com/r/piracy-gulf-guinea/

sticky to walk on, squishing with each step. Nevertheless, they are seeing a depletion of their quality of life while someone somewhere is making a lot of money. That builds resentment.

A poor, rural area along the coast where food sources are dwindling creates a vulnerable population with access to high-value oil and is a prime place for terrorists to come in and recruit for their cause. Terrorists bring money, supplies, and hopes for a different future, which the vulnerable population grabs onto as a glimmer of hope for a better tomorrow.

While there are many terrorist organizations believed to be involved in the rural Niger delta, one that stands out from the others is Boko Haram, also known as the Islamic State in West Africa (ISWA) and Islamic State's West African Province (ISWAP). Boko Haram was founded in Nigeria in 2002 by Muhammed Yusuf. Boko Haram is responsible for many assassinations, kidnappings, and large-scale acts of violence in Nigeria. When they formed Boko Haram, the intent was to uproot the corruption and injustice in Nigeria. In addition, they blamed the western influences for the deterioration of Nigerian culture, which contributed to the significant division between the few rich and many, many poor[2].

It is widely believed that Boko Haram is entirely, or at least partially, responsible for the piracy in the Gulf of Guinea to support their organization. However, even if they were not accountable, they were not helping with the resentment of some locals towards westerners working for the major oil company, Chevron.

That resentment carried onto the vessels that hired locals who believed they were entitled to pay but did not necessarily accept the responsibilities and work that came with the pay. This crew was probably the worst in my 30 years as a Merchant Seaman.

I wasn't that surprised, to be honest. On my first trip to Nigeria years earlier with a different company, they cautioned me

---

2  https://www.britannica.com/topic/Boko-Haram

to trust no one in Nigeria. If they got their way and you asked nothing of them, they could be semi-professional. They would not perform a lot of work but would do some. The less you bothered with them, the more they knew their jobs. Even though they could do the job, they wouldn't.

Adding to that, Schlumberger contracted ABs from a mixture of five different African countries. They did not all get along, eat the same foods, or speak the same dialect. When it was meal time, this created challenges for the cooks. One night I was sitting on the bridge when one of the managers asked me to speak with him because he had received complaints about the cooking. I told him yes, and asked what the complaints were. He stated that his men were complaining that the American Captains and Engineers were getting special treatment with the food the cooks were preparing for us. I asked for a specific example. He said the cake served to Americans had icing, and the cake given to the crew did not have icing (frosting). I told him that was an easy fix.

I called the cook to the bridge and asked him to start putting the icing on the cakes he served for Schlumberger's men. The cook said, no problem. So twice over the following week, the manager came back. The first time he stated that the icing served on the cakes was too sweet. I said okay, and talked to the cook. Then the manager tells me his crew is complaining again. They would rather have cake with no icing.

I was not only a Captain but a babysitter! This type of complaining was a daily event.

There was a week when the local manager had to fly out to have a big meeting with the upper management of Schlumberger. When he returned, we sat down to review a list of complaints. One complaint was that the Schlumberger personnel were upset at having so many flies inside the ship, mainly on the second level where their living quarters were located. To that, I explained that when performing rounds, at least 2 or 3 times daily, I found the watertight door on their level that leads to the outside open. I explained that if the crew would choose to close their watertight door, I would just about bet him my paycheck that the fly problem would take care of itself at least 95%.

When working in Nigeria, safety precautions are often completely disregarded. For example, the US Coast Guard taught Hazardous Materials (HAZMAT) handling during an inspection. Still no change in the ABs.

One day while reviewing the cargo onboard and checking to ensure that the hazardous cargo was stowed and labeled correctly according to HAZMAT and the Code of Federal Regulations guidelines, I discovered two tanks of dangerous and highly explosive chemicals. Both tanks had big, gaping, rusted-out holes on the top where the tank had corroded around the fill cap. It eroded to the point where there wasn't even a cap left.

I called the manager on board and asked her if she had inspected the cargo. She stated no that she had one of her FRAC Masters do it. I then showed her the two tanks. The manager called her FRAC Master to come down and fix this problem.

Oh, he came down. So this idiot came and shoved some rags in and stuffed the holes in the tanks with rags.

I had no choice but to refuse the voyage that day. We spent a lot of time in port on this vessel.

While in port, we were allowed to enter the camp at the shipyard where we docked. There was a pool and a bar, so we would go swimming or shoot pool for fun. Sometimes we would go through the gates and into the village. Some crew members would go to church, and others would go to the local bush bar.

We always felt safe in the village, as everyone there seemed to love us. The children would always come screaming, "Oyibo, Oyibo, Oyibo," which means white man, happy to see our return. We would give candy to the children and take the time to play with them.

At the gate from the shipping area to the local village area, these sweet older women would set up to sell fruit, vegetables, and bread. I loved these older women; they always gave me hugs and drinks. It seemed like they would bring me peace.

What was a small amount of money to me was a lot of money to them. It was hard to believe that peace was just footsteps away from the ship. But it sure was nice. We also made sure to donate to the local church as a token of appreciation for welcoming us to the community.

I worked on this vessel ported in Lagos, Nigeria, until 2011.

## CHAPTER THREE

# Onne, Nigeria

I had left Shlumberger for Edison Chouest Offshore (ECO). ECO was known to have excellent ships, with much nicer living quarters and cooks. ECO ships ported in Onne, Nigeria.

In Onne, I quickly realized, as I did in Lagos, that work had to be the Nigerian way, which is not always regulated, or even legal. It was challenging for men with the calmest tempers (a group that does not necessarily include me). Getting a Nigerian to follow the laws and rules is virtually impossible. I have had some ABs from Nigeria that were very easy to work with, but that number is low.

One of the rules we are required to enforce is that everyone onboard must have a Transportation Worker Identification Credential (TWIC). TWIC is a common identification credential necessary for all personnel who need access to secure areas regulated by the Maritime Transportation Security Act (MTSA) without an escort. Additionally, the TWIC is required for all mariners holding the United States Coast Guard-issued credentials. As the ships we were operating sail under the American flag, they fall to the security requirements of the US Coast Guard. To obtain a TWIC, each potential mariner must pass a comprehensive background investigation. In addition, there are many elements of disqualification for a TWIC.

The US Coast Guard International Port Security Program (IPSP) requires a plan to address vulnerabilities and prevent dangerous people and things from accessing ships and ports to protect the people and the cargo. The best practices of IPSP include background checks for hiring and periodically repeated background checks.

Sadly, it is easy to produce false certificates and documents in Nigeria. ECO had to fire many crewmembers and officers due to fake documents and then paid millions of Naira (Nigerian currency) to end their contracts. Some of these men had been with ECO for 10-20 years!

I've seen erroneous licenses, college diplomas, passports, IDs, Seaman's Certificates (STCW), and more. Fake documents are standard in 3rd world countries. When the company gets caught up in a situation like this, it is due to inferior management demonstrating a lack of concern and professionalism. It also shows the greediness of the company to save money. I say that because Nigeria has auditors and employment agencies that distinguish between false and official documents. But, as with everything else, you have to pay for quality.

A new chief officer was assigned to come on board, and I checked his credentials and talked with him about the ship. First, he did not have the proper documentation to work on my boat. That particular vessel had a dynamic positioning operator, and he had never handled a ship with a Z-drive.

Z-drive is a rudderless vessel. The wheels short spin 360 degrees, and to steer it, you turn your control knobs in the opposite direction that you want to go. It is the opposite of a ship with rudders where you steer in the direction you want to travel. Z-drives will virtually spin the boat on a dime, whereas rudders usually only turn to a 45-degree angle, which makes your turning circumference much bigger.

After speaking with the man for some time, I called my Nigerian manager and told him that this man wouldn't work out. However, the manager said the man's documents checked out, and the man told his Agent that he had experience with a Z-drive. Okay.

Regarding the background check, the manager stated that the man's village chief highly recommended him, as he was a very good man.

I let the manager know that does not fly with me. He was a decent man, a Christian, and I am sure he was a good Father. So I asked my manager what a village chief knows about seamanship because all of that does not make a good seaman.

The lack of security checks and only hiring from certain villages is dangerous. I could easily say a particular man from my town is a very good man as I see him in church and talk to him now and again. But does that mean I know him? Does that mean he isn't going to board the ship – lose it – and kill someone? Or beat the shit out of the Captain? No. If one individual gets fired from work, his friends and family in the village will bring hostility to work with them in defense of the man.

Between February 28, 2011, to June 3, 2011, I worked and transferred between four different vessels.

On July 5, 2011, I took over as Master on the *C-Retriever*. The *C-Retriever's* overall length is 240 feet with a beam (width) of 56 feet across. She is an offshore supply vessel. The Captain that ran this ship before I did not take care of the vessel or the crew, which was a shame because it was a relatively young ship built in 1999. ECO had it equipped with the best equipment possible. It had multiple orthopedic watch standing chairs with joystick controls and two computers on each arm of the chair. In the wheelhouse were big screens for easy viewing of the current location, radar, and all. She had top-of-the-line accommodations for the crew to relax in. The sleeping quarters were bigger than on many other ships and well appointed, and there was an excellent kitchen for preparing three meals a day to eat in the very nice dining room. However, it was not kept up properly. It was so out of control that the crew was running the boat.

I quickly learned that when working in Nigeria, you had to be a tough and strong Captain, or everyone would run over you. Not that I was an easy man to 'run over' with my standing 6 feet 2 inches and weighing in around 265 pounds. Many found my physical stature intimidating. Nevertheless, I was going through crewmember after crewmember.

Nigeria is just a weird place. It is tough to judge a quality employee from a bad one. To do it right and keep everyone on a solid path, I would have to do evaluations at least weekly. Even with the assessments, getting rid of anyone or trying to discipline anyone was difficult. These guys would perform like professional seamen one day, then wake up the next, not knowing the bow from the stern. WTF?

It always amazed me. I understand good days and bad days, but this was different. Way different.

On top of personnel issues, there were the challenges of various weather conditions. It was always a tough time in the winter. If it wasn't rough seas and weather, then it was fog. It was hard on the nerves to pilot the ship in foggy conditions. The thick rolling fog would sneak up and, at times, smother our vessel in a milky whiteness, destroying visibility. Yet, as a Captain, you never knew what dangers lurked in the fog. Therefore, during fog I kept my eyes glued to the radar – no daydreaming during that time.

On November 17, 2011, our ECO and Onne sister ship, the *C-Endeavour*, was near the Chevron Abgami oil field about 70 nautical miles offshore from Bayelsa State when eight Nigerian Pirates boarded the ship, attacking the crew and taking three hostages. Two of the hostages were Americans. The hostages gained release after fourteen days of negotiations.

We all knew that working in this area was risky, that the Nigerian pirates were boarding ships to steal cargo and, in some cases, take hostages. American hostages were big targets for the Nigerian pirates. Based on the belief that American companies could afford to pay high ransoms for hostages.

In 2009 Nigerian pirates attacked or attempted to board 28 different vessels. In 2010 that number was 19, and 2011 ended with ten boats. In 2012 the number of ships overtaken or that pirates attempted to board increased to 27, and in 2013 it was 18 vessels.

In June 2012, an incident in the wheelhouse with one of my ABs turned into a heated argument. My Nigerian mate should have stepped in and assisted me. However, he just stood there listening and taking it all in. Two ABs were assigned to the bridge to help the Captain or chief officer, whichever was on duty.

The two ABs assigned to the bridge that day were whispering and making cell phone calls while on watch. I asked them both to quit whispering because the sound was annoying. I told them if they wanted to speak privately, to talk in their native tongue, which I do not understand. They continued whispering back and forth and talking on their cell phones, so I told them to stay off their phones when they were on watch.

At that point, they started arguing with me. So I told the ABs to step outside the wheelhouse and talk if they wanted to keep up with the whispering. Then things heated up between us. I told them I would write them up if they continued to argue.

The statement that followed was so incomprehensible. Unbelievable. But true. One of the ABs stated very clearly that I was in Nigerian waters and that he would have me taken care of; because he was from the Niger Delta.

Still, my Nigerian mate said nothing. Thanks for the backup. I wrote up the AB, but I didn't have him sign it due to the security aspects of the situation. When we got back to port, I released him from the vessel.

After that event, I was boarded twice by Nigeria's equivalent of our Drug Enforcement Administration (DEA). When they were boarding, the Agents stated they received a report that I was dealing drugs from the ship. Of course, the allegation was crazy fabricated bullshit. However, they still thoroughly tossed my and my American engineer's rooms. They emptied every drawer and cupboard, flipped all furniture, and showed no care for our possessions. They just tore apart our rooms.

I always found it strange that they never looked in any Nigerian's rooms, only ours. However, they did find something – they found my Ex-Lax for constipation. Unfortunately, the Agents interpreted the label where it says it is a "stimulant" to mean it was a steroid. I told the Agent that if I were him, I would go home and take 2 or 3 of them and then go to the gym a couple of hours later.

The Agents were very unprofessional. I believe they had been paid to harass my engineer and me.

As the season changed into winter, rough seas were the norm. The ship bobbed up and down, rolling side-to-side as the angry, dark rolling waves with their white peaks slammed into the ship's side, spraying water across the deck. Heavy winds accompanied the angry waves. The rain created a gray mist that merged with the ocean spray diminishing visibility. When I was younger, I would get seasick when the seas were so rough. The rough seas are challenging for a different reason now; as a Captain, I know there are dangers around every corner.

One of the most tricky challenges in the rough weather was the expectations of the drilling rig company men. They would want the products and supplies we were delivering to be unloaded, even during the harsh conditions. So we did what we needed to do to get the job done.

As 2013 started, I continued to experience challenges with the ABs assigned to the ship. If you didn't do what they wanted, the same crew that worked well yesterday would all act like green deckhands today. For example, I overheard a 2nd engineer tell the chief engineer that he didn't know how to change a light bulb. He claimed this was because neither the chief nor the Captain would do what the crew wanted them to do.

After loading fuel, I left one dock and headed to another with the fuel adjuster on board. We heatedly argued, and I asked him to leave my wheelhouse. All I could think of was the 2012 incident all over again. Arguing on the bridge is not good. It's a significant security breach. Once I got the ship secured at the dock and called my manager, company security officer, and Chevron's Area manager.

Chevron's area manager came to the boat and had him removed and then discussed the situation with me. Of course, I was automatically at fault for being American and the other guy being Nigerian.

A few days later, my manager told me that Chevron wanted me off the ship. My manager told me no way it would happen. He assured Chevron that I was correct in handling the situation and that Chevron needed to act on it. He also told them they needed to back up any Captain removing someone from the bridge. My manager told me I was one of the Nigerian fleet's best and most professional, Captains.

On one of my trips, I was outbound from Onne, Nigeria, across Bonny Town, Nigeria, headed to Agbami oilfield, located on the Bonny River, with a cargo load. I was on the bridge preparing to take over the watch from my chief officer when a call came over the VHF radio. The man on the radio asked if Captain Wren Thomas was on board. After hearing him speak, I knew it was the mate that I had recently fired. Before I could say a word, my chief officer told him I was on board.

It was very suspicious to me because the mate on the radio didn't ask how I was doing and didn't ask to speak to me. Finally, he ended the radio transmission with an okay and thanked my chief officer.

After spending about a week offshore in Agbami field offloading cargo and pumping drilling materials, fuel, water, etc., we headed back to port. I received a call on the vessel's Nigerian cell phone when we arrived. I did not immediately recognize the voice but noticed he was Nigerian with a very educated voice.

The man told me I would be killed if I did not leave Nigeria immediately. He went on to say that if I ever returned to Nigeria, I would be killed.

I called my Nigerian mate to the bridge and explained what had happened. I asked him to call the number back, as it had come up with caller ID. My mate did this and was told by the man to stay out of it.

I called my senior manager and explained to him what had happened. He asked if I could think of who it could have been, and the only person I could think of was the mate I had fired recently. My manager, in turn, told me that if I wanted, he would get me out of the country. But, if he did that, the ship would be on downtime until he could get a replacement Captain. My manager reassured me that he would look into the phone call and take care of it. So I decided to stay on the vessel and keep the ship working so that the company didn't lose a lot of money.

Throughout the night, my manager and I spoke many times, with him telling me to go to bed and try to get some rest. I had given him the telephone number that called me, and he worked with Nigeria's SSS (their version of the CIA). Soon after, my manager told me they had found the phone number registered to the AB I had fired and that the SSS had arrested him. Knowing this reassured me that I should be safe. But unfortunately, these threats were only some of what I experienced.

Every foreigner is threatened as soon as they arrive on a ship in Nigeria. I won't say what these threats are because I want to protect my fellow seamen still working there. But I can say that it starts at Chevron Nigeria, Nigeria's Navy, INTELs personnel, and Mobile Police, to name a few.

Shortly after this incident, I went on my forty-five days off at home.

When I returned to Nigeria, I met a new Nigerian chief officer assigned to my ship. The man knew the electronics of operating the vessel but lacked in all other areas. I had a nickname for this chief officer; I called him pajama man. He would walk around off watch and come on watch wearing the same white pajamas every night. In addition, he would wear the long white cotton stocking cap.

One morning, while we were still in port, I was up on the bridge around 9:00 a.m. when I noticed that the crew wasn't doing any work, so I asked the chief officer what his plans were for the team that day.

He replied, "Capo, you didn't tell me to have them do anything."

There is always work on a vessel, especially one as large as the *C-Retriever*. For example, the crew could be cleaning, busting rust, or painting. So I asked him again, "Chief, why do I have to tell you what needs to be done? You are the chief officer. You should know what needs to be done. The only time I should have to tell you anything is if I want a particular project done."

Then I told him, "Get the men off of their cell phones and find something for them to do."

He didn't like this but went down to the main deck and had them work on our cargo rails. I thought good. Finally, they are doing something. They had gotten two electric grinders with wire wheels attached and began working on the racks busting rust.

After about fifteen minutes, I noticed it was pouring down rain. Thinking smart, I looked on the back deck, and low and behold, I was correct. The two deckhands were still grinding rust in the rain with electric grinders. I looked to my chief officer. He is kicked back in his chair in his usual white pajamas, with his feet up on the glass, talking on his cell phone, and wearing that stocking cap.

At that point, I lost it. I yelled, "Chief, what's the deal? Get off your cell phone and stop those two guys before they kill themselves."

We had a second or third mate sitting on the main deck doing a gangway watch, so now we had two officers watching these two dumbasses trying to kill themselves.

Knowing my chief officer was pissed at how I talked to him, I asked him if he had something he wanted to say.

He told me, "Captain, you need to understand that you are in Nigeria and that we do things differently in Nigeria than you do in the States."

I was like, unbelievable! I cannot believe this idiot just said that. The only response I could muster up was, "Whelp, I guess water and electricity mix in Nigeria."

I told our Nigerian Safety officer, Nigerian crew coordinator, and even our Nigerian area manager about it. After all that, the same chief officer still has never been written up for it, talked to about it, and was not fired. Last I knew, he still held the same position. I should have written him up, but at that point, I had written up, fired, and pissed off so many people that I wanted to see how the office would handle it.

He was a piece of shit, one of the laziest, most unprofessional men with whom I have ever worked. But I have to give him credit. He could handle the ship when he was paying attention.

## CHAPTER FOUR

# Trip Home

My next time home was from September 4 until October 8, 2013. I was helping a friend put on the metal siding for my cousin's new pole barn. I had a text from one of the managers that there was a problem and I needed to call him.

I was shaken to my core when I called and heard what he had to say. Someone in Nigeria, one of my crewmembers past or present, sent him an anonymous email saying that I always referred to the Nigerians as black monkeys. That I was dealing drugs and that I was participating in the illegal oil theft business.

I knew this was complete bullshit. So I told my manager to let me know who it was so that when I returned to Nigeria, I could confront the person in the presence of one of the managers in Nigeria.

My manager told me that he would have terminated the person immediately, as he knew the allegations were bullshit, if only he knew who it was. However, there was nothing either of us could do, as it had been sent anonymously with a fake email address (supposedly).

While I was home, I had this 6th sense feeling that something terrible would happen during my next work period in Nigeria. I knew tensions were high with some crew members, up to government officials, as I wasn't cooperating the way the Nigerians wanted me to.

I was on edge, and my friends and family knew it. They all could sense that something was wrong, that I was always deep in thought, and my mind was 1,000 miles away, with no ability to concentrate, and it worsened after the email to my manager.

I would often go to visit Mom and Grandma. Mom lived with my Grandma to care for her and the house chores.

One thing that I did while I was home was I decided to stop smoking. I went to the doctor and got a prescription for Wellbutrin to help block the nicotine cravings to assist me in quitting smoking. Wellbutrin is also an anti-depressant, but I wasn't taking it for that purpose then.

I don't know why I returned to Nigeria. I just knew it was my job, I'm an excellent Captain, and my company needed me. So I thought I just had to face my fears of going back.

## Captain Wren Thomas' Mother, Judy Davis-King

*I had noticed that he seemed stressed out the last several times when Wren came home. He knew there were problems in Nigeria but did not want us to worry, so he kept it to himself. Then, when it was time to return to work, he would stop every time on the way to the airport to tell his Grandma and me goodbye.*

*The last time he left, I could tell by the expressions on his face that something was really bothering him.*

*His Grandmother said, "Tommy, I wish you would not go back over there."*

*He said, "I know, Grandma." He hugged and kissed us, then left.*

## Captain Wren Thomas

I knew the dangers of Nigeria, but I knew my company needed me. I'm a US Merchant Seamen, and this is what I do.

## CHAPTER FIVE

# Return to Nigeria

When I arrived back in Nigeria and spoke with the off-going Master, he told me the mate he had was glad we were not going to crew change offshore. Then he said the mate did not want to ride with me back to shore. I knew right then my instinct was right. Something was going to happen.

My usual chief engineer was out on leave, so I had another American on board as chief engineer. I gave him his nickname HiLo the first time we worked together. He once asked how I came up with that nickname, and I told him I was tall, and he... wasn't. So I'm high, and he's low.

On October 17, 2013, we received an email from one of our warehouse managers stating that a group had threatened ECO from Bayelsa State, Nigeria. The threat indicated that if ECO did not start employing more people from Bayelsa, they would be attacking ECO vessels, kidnapping the crews, and burning the ships. In the company email, we were directed to revert to our vessel security plans if something should happen.

There went that feeling again. I just knew something was going to happen.

I called to talk to our warehouse manager about it, knowing Agbami wasn't far from Bayelsa. He assured me that the militants would most likely wait the two weeks. So trusting his judgment and not receiving an email from our home office or company security officer, I didn't worry about it too much.

I did decide it was best to have a security drill before our next run.

## CHAPTER SIX

# Voyage Thru the Badlands

We made four or five successful runs back to back to Agbami. No problems. I was almost starting to relax.

We were in port on October 21, 2013, when I received a phone call from Chevron's Area manager wanting to know how long it would take us to run to the Mere Field. My chief officer was up and took the call.

Three of us, my chief officer, chief engineer, HiLo, and I all found this run very unusual. We never made this run. Also, Agbami's other boat, the *C-Endeavour*, was still on drydock, so by taking this run, we were leaving no vessel to support Agbami.

We plotted out a course, making sure that we stayed a safe distance offshore. I even loaded the waypoints for the voyage into our GPS, so we would have that done when we were ready to leave for Mere.

I called our Chevron representative and gave him a run time for the voyage and an estimated arrival time (ETA). I also voiced my security concerns, especially after ECOs threat and knowing that this run would bring us close to the Bayelsa State. I was assured that a bourbon vessel had been making this run frequently and that I had nothing to worry about, as that vessel had never had any problems.

During the night, they loaded cargo for Mere Field. I spent the night reviewing our voyage plans and catching up on logs. Sometime between midnight and the morning of October 22, they also loaded a grocery box and a freezer container for a vessel in Pennington Field, which would bring us twenty-five nautical miles (nm) from the coast of Bayelsa State and the Port of Brass. This area is known as the "badlands" and is where most kidnappings occur.

There was no notification that they had added Pennington Field to our run until we received the paperwork for the run. I awoke that morning around 6:00 a.m. as it took two people and the chief engineer to get through the craziness of Chevron's paperwork and fuel soundings (measuring each tank and totaling the amount of fuel).

Then we received a box containing a radioactive source around 8:50 a.m., only ten minutes before the vessel convoy would leave. This addition to the ship's cargo added to the already boiling-over stress levels. At that point, I felt it was pertinent to argue with the Chevron representative that it was unacceptable to change this run with such short notice, giving me no time to plan.

All of my objections were overruled. I was forced to go. Chevron would not take no for an answer. "Trust us. Everything will be okay." Even after I said that this run would make the *C-Retriever* a sitting duck for pirates and hijackers. So I had to make this run.

If I had more time to plan, I would have discussed this with my office. But, again, this would not have helped. They would have gotten with Chevron, who would promise a security escort to meet us offshore. But magically, that security escort would have never shown. I have been there and done that already.

Before we left, I was drug into another argument, this time with the beach master in charge of the port's docks. The beach master wanted to know our voyage plans, cargo, and the number of passengers. After the attack and kidnapping on the *C-Endeavour* two years prior, I refused to give this information for security reasons. After all, it is common knowledge that the "bad guys" would listen in on this VHF radio conversation.

We have repeatedly complained about the beach master asking for this information in several safety meetings with Chevron. Giving this information to beach masters was dangerous and could lead to more and more attacks by giving the "bad boys" all of the vessel's information. Chevron's answer to me was, okay; we will write this up in our little notebook of "The Captain is bitching again" and would bring it up to the Captain of the Port.

The Chevron manager would also tell me, "Captain Wren, I beggo please understand that the beach masters are not very educated."

It's always puzzled me why Nigerians would put personnel in positions without proper training. Of course, I fully understand that everyone needs a job, and I respect that. But at the same time, I would not want the cable guy or a ship captain doing brain surgery on me.

Back to this trip, the beach masters argued over the radio, which was odd considering they knew I always told them to get with Chevron on the specifics because of security. But they still asked me and, on this day, argued quite heavily. I found this very odd. Of course, we would always have to tell the beach master no, but they always accepted it without argument.

So I argued over the VHF radio with the beach master telling him he needed to ask Chevron where we were headed. But then the beach master told me he knew where I was going. Then the beach master proceeded to broadcast our voyage plans, cargo, and the number of passengers over the radio. So our voyage details were out on the air for everyone listening on the VHF radio on the same channel to hear!

We departed Onne on the morning of October 22 with two

Americans and eleven Nigerians. The ship loaded with groceries, supplies, and a radioactive source going to Mere Field.

I was very concerned about the radioactive source on board. While going through radioactive training, we were informed that the last time a radioactive source went missing in Nigeria, it was recovered at Heathrow Airport in London, England. An other good reason for better security.

I continued to send emails throughout my day, even during my off-watch hours, stating my concerns. But unfortunately, I did not get any replies from Chevron. My nerves were on end, and my crew knew it.

**Deep in my gut, I knew I wasn't returning to port aboard my vessel. I knew tonight was the night I may not be going home.**

I had security meetings and talked to my crew about the dangers of this run. I stressed that they needed to be very vigilant during their watches. I told them to do no work except look out for the "bad boys."

I contemplated turning off the ships' running lights but chose not to because of regulations to have them on during low visibility. Having them on is dangerous, but having them off can be even worse as there are so many small boats running offshore with no radar. A collision is all I needed.

I took over on the Bonny River around 11:45 a.m. in front of Bonny Town and continued my run, still sending emails, while my mate watched the helm. My two ABs took their watch, one in the back of the wheelhouse standing lookout aft and one up forward standing lookout. It was the usual, "Hey men, turn off your cell phones – you're on watch."

I was too stressed to eat my lunch, which was out of character. During the next twelve hours, I worked plotting positions and talking with my crew. It was a quiet night with no engine room alarms and not too much offshore traffic. Finally, my chief officer and the rest of the midnight shift crew came to the bridge around 11:15 – 11:30 p.m. After all his men were on the bridge, I had a verbal safety meeting with them and handed over the night vision binoculars. It was a very nervous and very stressful pass-over with my chief officer.

CHAPTER SEVEN

# The Attack

## October 23, 2013

I decided it was time to try and get some sleep. I was exhausted due to my fluctuating blood pressure over the past two days. I again stressed to the crew and my officers to keep vigilant during their watch. To do nothing but watch. Usually, one of the deck crew would do their sanitary jobs: sweeping, mopping, and cleaning the heads (restrooms) on their assigned level.

I told them we would be going through the badlands right off the coast of Bayelsa State and arriving or being close to reaching there during their watch, which would have put us at Pennington Field between 9:00-12:00 a.m. on October 23. They knew I was serious, and all told me yes, sir.

Lying in bed, unable to sleep, I watched some TV and ate my pretzels, just waiting for the knock on my door that we were under attack. I was that sure that this was the night.

I'm not sure when I fell asleep, but the knock finally came around 3:00 a.m. It was HiLo, my chief engineer, and he was frantic! So this was it, I thought. I could see it in his eyes and heard it in his voice. He was serious. He told me they were on-board, and we had to get to our secure area now!

I knew what I needed to do; press our panic button on the

bridge, try to get a MayDay call out on the VHF radio, and maybe a call to our company security officer. That is what we did when we had security drills.

Now that it was happening, I was standing there stunned in my undershorts.

I quickly grabbed up a pair of dirty Levi's, and we ran to the engine room. When we arrived in the secure area, we locked down the hatch and did a headcount. We were missing three crew members. What do we do now? We talked about it and decided to stay put and pray that the missing three were tucked away somewhere and would not be found.

I debriefed my chief officer in the secure room and found out he did not press our panic button in the wheelhouse. I did not press the one in my room as I didn't know that it had been repaired after being found disconnected by one of our service techs.

I can't recall if we could secure our watertight door going into the engine room. But, if we could, I am not sure why it wasn't locked. I think the office had never put a locking pin on this door because it was inside the vessel.

I assumed we would have had little freeboard with the ship traveling less than ten knots. (Freeboard is what they call the part of the hull that is exposed. It is part of the hull between the main deck and the water's edge. So if you can see three feet of height from where the water stops on the hull to the top of the main deck, then it is said you have three feet of freeboard). So the pirates must have come alongside and crawled up the aircraft tires that the ship had on its side to act as bumpers.

The Nigerians have extraordinary physical abilities to climb. Nigerian Pirates were very athletic, agile, young in their 20's, and highly trained.

If they are determined and have the opportunity, there is not much you can do to stop them from getting on board. You can put barbed wire all over the place. You can put hinges on outside staircases and raise the stairs to keep them from walking up to them. I have also seen ships with tall chain link fencing, and none of this works, and none of this will work. It may slow their roll, but it doesn't stop them.

They were 100% prepared to accomplish their mission. The tools they carry with them are grapple hooks with lines attached and probably twelve-foot ladders and hooks on the top end of them to curve around the edge. These ladders are hung on a handrail, and the intruders climb up. And, of course, they had their guns. With the agility of these Nigerians, I can see how easy it would be to board us. After all, I'm 48 years old and could have done it with some difficulty, but I could have done it.

Figuring out that the chief officer had left the vessel on autopilot, I had my chief engineer take the controls back to the engine room, taking it from autopilot and slowing the ship to a speed consistent with the current. Now all we could do was wait. After a short time, my engineer came up with a good idea. He went to his controls and started spinning the ship in circles, hoping to attract attention.

We would open a little blower hatch to get more oxygen and spy on the pirates. We could see the pirates and confirmed they were armed with guns – locked and loaded. It was hot as hell in our safe room. After all, our 'safe room' was an equipment room, not an actual citadel as is found on some ships. It's stunning how much a company can spend on four or five orthopedic watch standing chairs, running upwards of $250,000 or more each. Yet, they will not pay any money to stop pirates or create a citadel.

Now we were locked into the bulk tank room (the engine room to the front and the z-drive room to the back). The pirates had two ways to access us: the watertight door, which divided the engine room, or the emergency escape hatch in the z-drive room. It was a metal cave-like room, with continual waves of heat rolling off the heavy-duty engine equipment. I was exhausted and thirsty; all I wanted to do was sleep. Nevertheless, I figured we would be safe, and rescue was soon to come.

I would lie on the deck in front of a portable blower to try and cool off and relax. But, it was so hot and sticky being sealed up in this metal cave. My adrenaline was pumping, sweat was seeping out of every pore, and the sweat was streaming down my body. The sweat was dripping down my head and hitting my glasses, so I had to continually take them off, wipe off the sweat and try to clean the lenses before putting them back on. Then the sweat would pour off my head and into my eye, the type of sweat that stings and burns a little when it hits your eye. It was miserable in there. My oiler, Bola, was doing a good job watching through the blower hatch. Finally, however, I had to take the advice of my crew.

They told me, "Captain, it will be over soon. The pirates will leave at daylight." I soon found out they were wrong. After about an hour, we started getting very thirsty. Sure it was probably from the stress and excitement, but it was that thirst you have to quench. Like the cotton-ball mouth when your tongue is so dry that it's sticking to the roof of your mouth or the back of your teeth, and you can barely form words. So I decided to risk it and drink water from the hose. The pirates tried their best to open the hatch using hammers. They beat on it, trying to break the wheel that secures the door by spinning rods into place. The revolution was blocked by a bolt that we put in place to keep them from spinning the wheel. It acts as a stopper.

After a couple of hours, the pirates somehow found a mini-grinder equipped with a cutting blade capable of cutting through steel, and they used it. They were cutting away at the steel hatch. A loud, continual, screeching metal-on-metal sound echoed in our metal cave as the blade worked its way through the steel and my nerves. When we saw the edge coming through the steel hatch, I knew it wouldn't be long before they had us.

When they cut a fairly good-sized hole into the door, all I

could do was fight. I pulled out the garden hose from which I had been drinking water and sprayed water at the pirates through the hole. I was hoping to electrocute them or at least slow them down. Instead, the pirates were screaming at us to stop spraying the water and give ourselves up, and we would not be killed.

I was fighting to stop them as they were fighting to get in. I put metal flange covers in the doors locking bars to slow their progress. While I was doing this, HiLo, my chief engineer, was at his controls spinning the ship in circles hoping to attract attention.

After about an hour of screeching, grinding, and cutting, they finally had a decent-sized hole. The pirates beat the hole with a sledgehammer, which made it bigger until it was large enough to get their hands through to move the flanges. Then they stuck the barrel of an AK-47 through the hole and fired rounds into our room. Each shot sounded like a compression bomb going off inside the engine room, followed by some very dangerous tink, tink, tinking noises as bullets ricocheted across the room. If they didn't get us with a direct shot, the ricochet was not something we could avoid long.

I walked to the back of the room to find HiLo and my crew. My crew was gone. They vanished. They were hidden, and they were not coming out. I told my chief that this was pucker time. We only had two choices; give ourselves up or take the chance of the pirates firing more rounds into the room and possibly killing us. They would have had an excellent chance of killing us because each pirate had three thirty-round clips taped together, and that's a lot of bullets.

We both agreed that it was time to give ourselves up and save our crew and possibly prevent more damage to the ship. So we both walked to the door. I screamed to the pirates that we were coming out, not to fire.

We had spent over six hours in a sweltering, water-sealed tank room. At the same time, half a dozen pirates stormed the ship and began their siege. They were specifically looking for their prize: the American Captain and his American Engineer.

Before they started cutting through the door, I was lying on the deck plates waiting for the cavalry to arrive and worrying about the fate of the crew members that didn't make it to the safe room with us. As I slowly opened the door, I saw my second engineer lying on the deck and the fright in his eyes. He looked unharmed but terrified.

The two pirates there walked us up to the main deck and outside. They demanded to know where the rest of the crew was.

I told him, "How should I know?"

If he wanted them, he would have to find them.

At this point, I was in survival mode and pissed! He kept demanding that I give up the rest of the crew, and I wouldn't. He wasn't getting anyone but my chief engineer and me.

As pissed as I was, I decided it was best to control my temper and try to gain some trust. I did this by treating the pirate as if I was on his team. We talked for a few minutes, with the leader arguing back and forth with two other pirates, wanting to leave the vessel.

I finally persuaded him to let me grab my medications. Then, the pirate leader declared that I looked like the World Wrestling Federation / World Wrestling Entertainment (*WWE*) professional wrestler Stone Cold Steve Austin and proclaimed he would call me Stone Cold Steve Austin.

He escorted me to the bridge, and I looked around in absolute disbelief. Annihilated is the word that comes to mind to describe the bridge. There was glass everywhere, and as far as I could tell, every electronic screen, monitor, or device was damaged or destroyed. In addition, they had shot out the window next to the watertight door that leads into the bridge's aft.

We then continued down to my stateroom, and it had been ransacked. So was HiLo's room. HiLo had locked his stateroom door before he went down, so the pirates had to destroy the door vent and reach inside to unlock it. All I could think to do was grab a suitcase, throw some clothes in it, and what medicine I could grab. I grabbed every can of Skoal I had and what clothes they didn't already steal. Unfortunately, they had taken every pair of my underwear.

While I was doing all of this, my escort told me –

"You work for Chevron, yes?"

I told him yes, and he was right that we work for Chevron.

We then walked back to the wheelhouse and down to the main deck. As we walked through the demolished wheelhouse, I grabbed a bottle of Doxycycline (an antibiotic we took as part of our Anti-Malaria program) and, I think, the bottles of Advil and Tylenol. Later I thought about it, and I wish I had grabbed the first aid bag. There was a bag with first aid supplies and two first aid kits. I didn't sweat it; I was happy I could get what I did.

## CHAPTER EIGHT

# Taken Away from Ship

The time had come. Just after 9:00 a.m. on October 23, they forced me to leave my vessel at gunpoint. A moment no Captain ever wants to face. But there was no other reasonable option, die or be kidnapped by the pirates. So the pirates forced me and my chief engineer, HiLo, to board their old, small, gray-looking fiberglass speedboat, which was tied to the *C-Retriever*. The boat is the type regularly used for fishing in African countries. So now it is me, HiLo, and six armed pirates heading to God-knows-where in this little boat.

Getting underway towards north-northeast, we sailed for probably an hour. The pirates were excitedly talking to us, asking questions about our company and if we thought the company would pay 200 million Naira ($4,625.67 US dollars) in ransom for us. It seemed for the moment that their goal was the money and not to kill us.

While we were sailing, we came across a shrimp boat. The shrimp boat was much larger than the fiberglass boat we were in and had several deck mates onboard, along with the Captain. As we got alongside the shrimp boat, two of the pirates started screaming at the shrimp boat Captain to stop his boat. Then, the pirates started firing their weapons when the shrimp boat didn't stop. The shrimp boat Captain finally stopped his craft, and his men on deck threw a small line for the pirates to tie off, connecting the two boats.

With the line secured, two pirates climbed aboard the shrimp boat. After they were onboard the shrimp boat, the pirates threw a more significant one-and-a-half-inch line to the pirates in our ship to tie to the speedboat's bow. Once that was secure, the much larger and more powerful shrimp boat started towing us towards the shore.

Watching the shrimp boat and what was happening, I noticed that the two pirates on the shrimp boat started getting agitated. They began beating the deckhands with the butts of their rifles. They were not satisfied until one of the pirates handed his rifle to the other and began beating the men with a board he found on the boat.

Sitting and watching what was happening on the shrimp boat, HiLo and I looked at one another. We exchanged a look of grave concern. It was a scary scene, not knowing what had triggered the pirates to beat the deck mates. However, it seemed we were both thinking the same thing, that we did not want to set off this out-of-control reaction from the pirates.

The time of day was a bit of a blur, as the skies were clear and sunny with no clouds, and the temperature continually increased to become hotter and hotter. The swells in the ocean were between five to eight feet. Every wave the boat hit showered us with burning saltwater, reminding us that with no hats and wearing short sleeve shirts, both HiLo and I were sure to burn in the sweltering sun. The saltwater was everywhere, in our eyes and skin, helping our clothes stick to our bodies.

After an hour of being towed, the two ships stopped, and the pirates returned to the small fiberglass boat. They returned with the money, food, and bottled water they had stolen. Then, our ship headed off without the shrimp boat because the shrimp boat's engine had failed.

We sailed for about another hour and came across another large shrimp boat. Again, the pirates went through the same process of yelling and shooting to gain the boat's attention. However, the second Captain was more intelligent and kept quiet, following the pirate's directions.

Once again, the pirates went through the process of tying off to the shrimp boat, boarding the ship, and tying off our bow to a thicker line. While we were alongside the second shrimp boat, I noticed that one of the deckhands was wearing a ball cap. I told the pirate, who seemed to be the leader, to get the ball cap from the deckhand.

He gave it to me, and I handed it over to HiLo because I could tell his bald head was getting sunburned. Our heads were severely sunburnt, which was very painful. I also had a headache and was concerned about the possibility of heat stroke.

Once the tow line was hooked up, we continued towards Brass.

## Captain Wren Thomas' Wife, Rhonda Thomas

## October 23, 2013

*I was out of sorts all morning. I hadn't felt right since Tommy (this is the family-only name for Wren) left a couple of weeks ago. There was just something "off." We talked every day either on the phone or on yahoo instant messenger. Sometimes we didn't connect until later in the day, but we always talked at least once daily.*

*Today I did my usual chores and went to work at the high school at 10:00 a.m. central.*

*At 10:04 a.m., my phone began to buzz, I looked at the number, and it was from Houma, LA; I already knew what they were going to say.*

*I stepped into the hallway and answered the phone. It was Stephen Bossier from Edison Chouest. His was not a name that I knew or recognized. I have met many of Tommy's bosses and talked with* him about many people in his company, but not this man. He told me pirates had attacked the C-Retriever at approximately 3:00 a.m. and that Tommy and his chief engineer had been kidnapped.

He gave me little details but provided his contact information and told me he would contact me again in an hour or two.

I told my boss, Kim, what was happening, and then told the Principal that I had to leave. When I left, I drove my car for what seemed to be an eternity. First, I headed toward Wren's sister Sheri's work, then changed my mind and headed toward his Mom's and his Granny's, then changed my mind again and drove to his sister Brenda's house. I was texting and calling Brenda as I went, but she didn't answer. When I arrived, she didn't answer the door at first, but I beat on the door until she did.

Once I told Brenda the news, we began calling other people. Brenda called his ex-wife Jenny so that she could tell Wren's sons, Blake and Dillon. I called my Uncle Denny. Brenda called her sisters Sheri and Kari while I called my sisters.

Before we left Brenda's to return to our home, she packed a bag to stay with me and my daughter, Ruby. All afternoon the calls were flooding in.

First was Joe from FBI Quantico and Tom, an FBI Crisis Negotiator. Then came Tom from the NY office of ECO. Next was Amie from the FBI Springfield office. She told me that she and a couple of her team members were coming to the house to talk to me.

After that, Terri from the State Department called, then Marjorie from the Pentagon. Everyone gave me their name and contact information.

I was trying to stay with my regular schedule and went to drive the school bus route that afternoon. On the way, I got a call from Kathy, FBI Springfield, and Kabri Aliyu from the Nigerian Navy. The next call was from a person who said they were with the IMO, but I didn't know that the IMO was International Maritime Organization.

All these calls and no one had any more information.

I went to pick up Ruby after work. I told her the story of what *happened. She cried hard and asked appropriate questions for a seven-year-old.*

*She said, "Please, Mommy, tell me that Tommy will come home and not be hurt."*

*When we arrived home, she went straight to her room and didn't come out for a while.*

## Captain Wren Thomas' Mother, Judy Davis-King

*As I drove to my house, I saw my daughter Sheri's car in the driveway. I wondered why she was here in the middle of the day; usually, she would be at work. But instead, she was standing as I came in the front door. She says, "Mom, maybe you should sit down. I need to tell you something."*

*My heart raced when Sheri said, "Mom, Tommy is okay, but he and his chief engineer have been kidnapped."*

*I went numb, sinking into my recliner. That's the last thing a mother wants to hear. All kinds of questions were popping into my head. Is he alright? Have they hurt him? Where did they take him? All sorts of questions, which no one had the answers to now. Did they take him out of Nigeria? God, is he okay?*

## Captain Wren Thomas

I don't know why we disconnected from that shrimp boat, but we did about an hour later. We pulled alongside; the two pirates rejoined our small speedboat with money, food, and water they had stolen. The pirates disconnected the line to the boat, and we sailed off.

Then there was a third large shrimp boat we came across about thirty minutes later. Again they were boarded, we were towed, and they were robbed. This time we were towed for approximately an hour. By then, the leader of the pirates indicated that he had regained his bearings and decided to disconnect and finish the voyage.

## Captain Wren Thomas' Son, Dillon Thomas

## October 23, 2013

*"Dill, you need to come over after work. We need to talk." My Mom never tells me this, so instantly, I know something is wrong. I kept trying to get her to tell me, but she wouldn't, so a million things were running through my mind as to what it could be. Did somebody die? Did somebody win the lottery? It could be good, and it could be bad.*

*About thirty minutes later, my Mom showed up at work and told me to get into the car. What she said next ended up being the longest day of my life.*

*Mom said, "Dill, your Dad has been kidnapped by pirates." I just sat there for the longest time. I couldn't believe it and didn't want to believe it. My Dad, "SUPERMAN," had been kidnapped by pirates. A person who would give the shirt off his back and socks off his feet to help people in need.*

*Mom didn't know any other details. Not knowing any details made me instantly mad at the world. My Father has been kidnapped, and I have no clue. It's like Usain Bolt; the fastest man ever was running laps in my mind.*

*Is he alive? Is he dead? Are they torturing him? Is his head sitting atop a pole with the Nigerians having a party around his head like some type of trophy?*

*I dropped to my knees and started crying and going into deep thought, thinking, this can't be real.*

*A few hours later, I got a call from the FBI. "Dillon, we are sorry to inform you, but your Father has been kidnapped. We're very sorry, but we don't know if your Father is dead or alive or if this is just a kidnapping for ransom or an act of terrorism."*

*At that point, I'm just hurt and angry. To think these people work for the Federal Government, and they can't tell me anything?*

## Captain Wren Thomas

As we approached the beach and the opening to the creek, HiLo and I were excited to see land and get out of the rough swells. Unfortunately, every time the boat hit a wave, we were soaked and beaten from the slamming down of the hull. As I stretched my legs, my jeans were plastered to my skin. Every movement made the seams of the denim chaffe on my legs and skin. My shirt stuck to my body, and I could feel the sunburn, especially when the saltwater hit my flesh and stung. I had long since given up on drying off my glasses; it just was not happening.

Looking around, I noticed a ship that had been blown aground. It was a cargo ship, probably about three hundred feet long, and it looked like a ghost ship just sitting there waiting. It was a sad sight, a massive hull out of the water, paint peeling where there was still paint, the rest of the ship covered in rust. It had been aground for a few years. Blown here from a storm or brought ashore riding the currents, most likely due to engine failure. So there she sat, half in and half out of the water, weeds growing up around it and on it. The ship looked tired and worn out. HiLo and I could relate to the vessel after being battered by the sea in the small boat for seven or more hours. We were soaked to the core from the waves beating down on us, showering us in salt water on top of some significant sunburns. On top of the physical were the mental concerns – we had been kidnapped.

## Captain Wren Thomas' Wife, Rhonda Thomas

*Stephen from ECO called me a few times during the day. I asked him, "Where is my husband?" "Is anyone hurt?" "What about the crew?" "Where is the ship?" Along with many other questions.*

*Stephen told me the crew was fine, and it took a few calls for me to understand that Tommy and his engineer had been removed from the ship and the crew was left behind. In addition, Stephen told me that the cook on the vessel sustained minor injuries when he was shoved and got a cut on his head, but there was no information that there were any other injuries.*

*Stephen told me that the communications systems were disabled, and there was a lot of damage to the vessel.*

*Around 4:00 p.m. central time, the FBI ladies showed up at the house, but they only had the same information I had gotten from Stephen. They got vital data on Tommy and obtained consent to monitor my communications with Tommy, past, and present. They stayed very late. It was almost midnight before they left.*

*I was disappointed and very frustrated with the lack of information and the phones constantly ringing all day. But now that Ruby was asleep, Brenda slept in Dillon's bed. I lay there looking at the ceiling, processing everything. I kept getting up and going to the patio door to see the moon, praying that Tommy was looking at it too.*

*Brenda was up and down throughout the night as well. We kept scouring the internet for information. Ruby woke up just about every hour to ask if they had found Tommy yet.*

## Captain Wren Thomas' Mother, Judy Davis-King

To the man you've become
and the son you'll always be.

*I lay in bed at night thinking back to when Wren was born and his years as a boy growing up. He always had a smile on his face. When he got into trouble, he stood there smiling, just grinning at me. That made it even harder to scold him.*

*Thinking back to when he was born on May 27, 1965, I had a very long hard delivery. He came out face up instead of face down. He ended up with a broken collarbone, and his face was badly bruised. I could hardly wait to take him home. Waiting at home was his sister Brenda, age five, and his sister Sheri age eighteen months old. They were so excited to have a baby brother. His Father was excited about having a son. We named him Wren Cole Thomas III. We nicknamed him Tommy. Most of us still call him Tom or Tommy.*

*After graduating high school, he moved to Louisiana to work as a deckhand with his cousin. That's when they started calling him by his first name. It didn't take him long to decide he would rather work offshore than in Illinois. So he went and applied for his seaman's documents.*

*He had left the offshore work and enlisted in the US Marines for some time. Once he was out of the Marine Corps, he returned to working offshore. It was where he wanted to be.*

*Over the years, he worked his way up the chain and studied to be a Captain. He is now known as Captain Wren.*

*As I lay in bed at night, I started reminiscing about his years at home. We lived in the small community of Sidney, Illinois, on four acres in an old two-story farmhouse at the edge of town. We had several horses and a donkey. Chickens were running all over the place. We loved our home and the small farm-type life. His Father was a plumber, and I was a stay-at-home mom. On Friday nights, we would go uptown to the small restaurant to eat. This one Friday night, my sister and her three children joined us. It was always fish night for ones who like fish. The kids usually wanted a hamburger and fries.*

*It was the night of October 18, l968, when Wren's Father got up from the table and ran to the restroom. My sister saw him get up, and there was blood running down his face. I jumped up too and went to see what was happening. He was hemorrhaging from his nose and mouth. My sister had her arms around his waist, holding him over the stool. I ran across the street to the doctor's office and cried for help. The ambulance finally got there, and when we got to the hospital, they told me he had died. He had a ruptured thoracic aneurysm on the main artery to his heart. He was only thirty-eight years old. Our son Wren was only three years old. I remember telling the doctor that all my husband ever wanted was a son; now, he could not live to see him grow up. It was pretty traumatic for the children to be sitting at the table when this happened.*

*When we were getting ready for the funeral, I was trying to get his dad's suit out of the closet for them to take to the funeral home. My son said, "Mommy are they going to put daddy on a stage? "Oh, did the tears run. After the funeral, his sister, age five, asked me if she could put a sign in the yard. She wanted a sign that said, "We want a daddy." She said Mommy, you have a wedding dress in the attic. More tears ran. My children were a reason to get out of bed each morning. As time went on, I finally remarried. The children were pretty much raised by their stepfather, Phil Richards, and me.*

*I had to realize that my son was a grown man. He was not the little boy who would run into the house if he got in a fight and locked the doors. He was a man now with no place to run. He was at the mercy of his capturers. I cannot even imagine the horror of the whole situation or what they may have had to endure.*

*I tried to keep my emotions intact when around the family so they would not have to worry about me. I live with my mother, who is ninety-one, and I did not want to upset her more than she already was. Tears flowed when I was in bed at night. Tears are supposed to be cleansing, so I needed that to get thru each day. I just wanted to hear his voice.*

*It was hard as he was always the one who had his hand out to*

*help everyone else. Caring for and doing for others was the thing
in life that he loved to do. But, our hands were tied when it was
our turn to help him. The only thing we could do for him was pray!*

## Captain Wren Thomas

As we continued past the abandoned ghost ship, we sailed into
the mouth of the creek. The boat we were in ran aground and
waited until it was pushed in with a swell. As soon as we were in
the creek, the leader made HiLo and I get down and covered us
with an old, smelly tarp they had in the boat.

They kept us hidden under this thick plastic that added to our
sweating in the humid air for quite a bit. So now we could not
identify landmarks to know where they were taking us. No idea
where they were headed, what they were going to do with us,
and who they were hiding us from – was it the Nigerian Navy,
other local pirates, or were we close enough to be seen by other
Americans?

After some time, the leader ordered us to come out from
under the tarp as we approached the camp. He was moving as
fast as the boat would go, and we finally arrived at the camp.

Upon our approach, we looked in amazement at the homemade pier they had built. I have no idea how this rickety pier was
even standing. Plank boards that seemed incredibly old, gray,
and weakened were lying across other planks that they had stuck
in the mud. Yet, it was full of jumping, screaming men with
rifles. They seemed as excited as someone who had just won a
multi-million dollar lottery.

As we pulled up alongside the pier, we were ordered, at
gunpoint, out of the boat. I started to think about my Marine
Corps training to assess our situation. And our situation was,
"We were FUCKED." Plain and simple.

## CHAPTER NINE

# First Camp

The camp was sitting in an opening about 200 feet wide and 75 feet deep. The ground was sticky mud, saturated with oil spill pollutants, water, and whatever else. It was the mud that would squish when you stepped. Then your foot would sink into the mud and hear a suction-like squoosh when you pulled your foot up for the next step. Mangroves surrounded two simplistic grass huts. The mangroves' thick, gnarled walking legs were so tightly interwoven that I don't think mosquitoes could have escaped through them. They created an insurmountable barrier to any escape attempt.

No escape route and no cover presented a considerable problem. We had no cover or concealment (nothing to hide behind when bullets start flying). Which sucked and was particularly scary. I knew that we were sitting ducks. The only thing we could have counted on was a team of Navy Seals coming in quietly and hitting fourteen bulls-eyes before our captors got off two shots of their own.

We could have tried to swim the Creek. But, well, we were lost with no bearings, and knowing nothing about these swamps meant swimming away was not an option. Well, it was an option, a suicide option. So we waited.

After our chaotic arrival at the camp, they escorted us into a hut with four walls and a roof. Inside the hut, they directed us to sit down on a bunk built from bamboo and an old piece of a foam mattress. At least we would be up out of the muddy ground. That would become our home away from home.

Once everyone was in the grass hut, all of the pirates who had been on the boat were searched to ensure they weren't holding onto anything stolen from the shrimp boats or our ship. There was no trust. Then the pirates and crew decided to divvy up the money. Throughout the ordeal, all I could tell they stole was a bunch of cell phones, a PDA-type notebook, and a Self-Contained Breathing Apparatus (SCBA) which was for fighting fires, but the leader said he was going to use it for diving as he was a diver.

In addition, they had stolen food, water, and a lead baby blue apron used for handling radioactive sources (basically the same type they use in hospitals). They also had my underwear, boots, tennis shoes, jogging outfits, and a silver cross my wife had given me.

I was surprised they didn't steal the more valuable, helpful stuff in the wheelhouse like VHF radios. However, they did manage to steal the 25 HP outboard engine off our rescue boat.

The main guy introduced himself. His name was Seamar, and he was the leader. Seamar was tall with a skinny face and kinky, coiled hair.

Next, we were introduced to Seaman, the second in command. We nicknamed Seaman 'Bubba' after Bubba in the movie "Forest Gump" because he looked just like Bubba. He had a round, boyish face like a 12-year-old but with the same hair as Seamar. Seaman was short and ugly. Uglier than a fence post type of ugly. Of course, he thought he was a real ladies' man. He was also psycho as hell. I guessed he would do anything he was asked to do, including killing us. I wasn't sure which one had the worse temper as we had witnessed both flying off the hook fast.

The crew had a spiritual leader who was known as Preacher.

There was a young community boy that took care of us named Dee. He was a cross between a helper and a slave of the crew.

There was another man they called Blackie.

There was a man with a prosthetic leg. We nicknamed him Storytime as he would always tell stories from the Bible to God knows what, and the higher he was, the longer the stories were. Storytime was a crazy man. He also appeared to be an expert with his French-made M-60. He would tell stories about Shadrach, Meshach, and Abednego being burned alive by being thrown into a fiery furnace from the book of *Daniel 3:13-28*. Then suddenly say, "They were not listening, and they fucked up immediately." He was psycho and another one to keep an eye on.

The rest of the crew didn't matter to me, so we had nicknames for them: the Singer, Talker, the Olympian, whatever. HiLo and I would make up whatever we could to make each other laugh. We would also rotate the names or change them. The main thing is that all of them appeared thin-built and athletic.

We were hungry, thirsty, tired, and needed a shower after being up since 3:00 a.m., hiding, then being taken off the ship and beaten by the swells for six or eight hours, shoved under a tarp, and then arriving here. We sat there, looking around and listening to all the sounds of the animals in the rainforest. All around us were various birds chirping, whistling, and crowing. It was an additional level of noise in our environment.

Then, the captors built a fire inside the hut under some bamboo that they used to create a makeshift smoker-style cooker. They were drying (smoking) the shrimp and fish they had stolen from the boats. They had stolen so much shrimp and fish that there was no way that it could all be eaten immediately.

We lay on our foam mattress where they directed us to sit. We watched and listened. Most of the captors cheered and partied, smoking pot and crack cocaine. We thought they were doing this in celebration of our capture.

The one good thing was that we had bottled water and were offered more bottles. We accepted them and drank as much as we could. I think the first day, I drank 3 or 4 bottles. I was greedy because I knew we would have it rough when the party started.

Seamar brought us outside the hut to talk to us. He told us if anyone tried to rescue us, they would kill us immediately because if they could not get ransom, then we were of no use to them. He then asked how long it would take for our company to get the ransom arranged. I told him and HiLo that we had at least a 14-day wait because that was how long it took to get the 2 Americans and 1 Mexican kidnapped from when our sister ship, the *C-Endeavour*, was attacked.

Back in the hut, they would play 4 or 5 cell phones at a time, with every one of them playing different music and a radio playing news. The range of music choices was bizarre, with one cell phone playing Dolly Parton's song "Coat of Many Colors" and another playing hip hop rap by 50 Cents. It made no sense. One of the songs they would play was a fast-moving tribal song, almost like disco. This song became known by us as the "Reefer Addict Song." These idiots would play it over and over and over. That song drove me bat shit crazy!

When we were inside, HiLo and I tried to get some sleep.

## Captain Wren Thomas' Wife, Rhonda Thomas

## October 24, 2013

*I got up and went to work while Brenda took Ruby to school. The news still hadn't started broadcasting stories about the situation. Then, the FBI ladies came back. Kathy gave me a phone recording device with instructions that if someone from the militant group contacted me, I would answer and record the call and refer my calls to the negotiating group. Kathy brought a Quantico t-shirt for Ruby.*

*I was sure that today we would hear more information. I certainly had more questions. Why didn't someone come to help them if they were on the ship being attacked for six hours? What was happening during those six hours? My sisters and Uncle Denny, Sheri, Kari, Judy, and Aunt Kay came over for more news.*

*The news broke when I did my afternoon bus run. It was first on G-Captain. Brenda and I both asked the FBI many questions, as these ladies were assigned to be our informational liaisons. They warned us about reading stories on the internet and negated most of what we asked. By evening, all major news outlets were broadcasting the report, over and over. Our eyes were glued to the television, hoping they would say something giving us more information than we had, even if it wasn't reliably sourced. I noted that Tommy and his chief engineer's names were not released.*

*I decided to reach out to Tommy's chief engineer's wife. At that time, I assumed the chief was Mike because Mike always works in Tommy's rotation. The FBI ladies said that they would make the request. Again the FBI ladies were at the house until very late.*

*That night Brenda was up the entire night again, with news story after news story hitting the internet. I was up the whole night reading, watching, and waiting. Ruby slept in my bed again and finally slept through the night.*

*Brenda had gotten up for a drink during the night, and I got up to look at the moon again, and she didn't hear me coming down the stairs, so we had a collision in the hallway and woke Ruby. Shoot, we yelled so loud we should have awakened the dead. Then we started laughing, and it felt good to laugh, if only for a minute.*

## Captain Wren Thomas

### The first week of captivity

I found a pen and a piece of cardboard and decided to use them to write down the days, and if there were ransom offers, I would take notes. The pen I found happened to be on a lanyard, and

I would spin it around my fingers for what seemed like hours. HiLo tells me, well, at least you have something to play with for 14 days.

HiLo and I wondered which country would send the cavalry for us first. Nigeria or the USA? I prayed every day for rescue, and every night I begged God to keep everyone away from us.

While sitting there, we traded many club stories as we both belong to motorcycle clubs. HiLo, the Sergeant at Arms in his club, and I am the Enforcer in mine, which is Stone Cold Motorcycle Club out of Champaign, Illinois. I can imagine it was a bit intimidating for the pirates looking at us, as we are both solid, muscular men who do not look like we tolerate a lot of crap. But, it gave us a bond. Being bikers, we knew the level of trust and brotherhood that came with that lifestyle.

On the 2nd day, we somehow managed to get some sleep and were permitted to shower. We walked out the back door and found a makeshift shower stall made of bamboo. It offered a little privacy. Our captors provided a bar of soap and a bucket of dirty river water. Although the river water was disgusting, getting the stink and dried salt water off our bodies felt good.

We dosed off just to be awoken about 7:00 p.m. by cell phone chaos and people screaming. But, of course, they were not screaming about anything in particular, just partying. So, while our captors were partying, HiLo and I took in the camp atmosphere.

When the pirates boarded the *C-Retriever,* they dressed poorly in scraggly clothes, too big for them, with the saggy bottom barely covering part of their butts. The clothes appeared like they had been stolen or otherwise acquired. In addition, they had rags tied around their heads and arms for some reason.

While in the camp, they would just walk around in my under drawers which they had stolen from my cabin. Seeing these pirates walking around in only my undershorts was an odd sight. While at camp, they were mostly barefoot. They had homemade web belt slings tied around the butt of their AK-47s. We also noted that they used what appeared to be duct or packing tape on the banana clips of their rifles, with the clips facing opposite directions for a quick reload. They kept their weapons on the homemade slings whenever they were awake.

When a group was leaving the camp, they would get dressed in their saggy shorts and whatever shirts they had. Some left barefoot, and others left wearing my boots and tennis shoes they took from my cabin.

Some of the captors had left camp with the money they stole from the shrimp boats and bought a generator, electric wiring, sockets, and lightbulbs. If the noise hadn't been bad enough already, they had a way to recharge their cell phones. One of the more intelligent pirates used the wire to string lights inside the hut and out the back to the shower area.

Also, on the second day, I heard something that upset me. The captors were talking in their native language, and the name Charles was mentioned. The only Charles I knew was Charles, who was the Nigerian manager in charge of Onne. After hearing so much, I knew, and no one could convince me otherwise, that someone had set up the *C-Retriever*. It made me think that our kidnapping was more extensive than people could imagine. It sucked that many people involved were people that I had trusted.

Sometime during these first few days, I contracted jock itch, which turned into what I refer to as jungle rot. It was bad. It was worse than anything I had ever had. It burned and itched 24 hours a day, with the nights being the worse. I had caught jock itch with the rest of my platoon during infantry school when I was in the Corps, and it wasn't nearly this bad.

The infection was so painful that I couldn't sleep because of the pain, and then I couldn't sleep because of the noise and music. I soon realized that sticking a dry t-shirt or water bottle between my legs would relieve me while sleeping.

I talked Seamar into going to town so he could buy me some

antibiotics or cream. I also told him I had asthma and needed a bronchial inhaler. I had one with me because I had just recovered from bronchitis a few weeks before. So I also asked him to pick up more inhalers I needed. I didn't need the inhalers, but I truly wanted this to cost him a lot of money, they had kidnapped the wrong American, and he soon found that out.

So he and some men got ready to go to town to get those items and other supplies. Before leaving, he took me outside and told me, "Mr. Stone Cold, when I return, you will be able to talk to your office."

He explained, "I have been waiting on my boss, but now I hear the boss has recently been captured and killed by the Nigerian government."

Seamar continued, "Mr. Stone Cold, my boss was a very good man. He was very handsome and generous, and we are only doing this because your company wasn't providing jobs. The government steals all the oil money and does not provide good schools, hospitals, roads, jobs."

## Captain Wren Thomas' Wife, Rhonda Thomas

### October 25, 2013

*It was too much. I couldn't keep working on no sleep. Jumping every time my phone rang, wondering if it was the kidnappers or my husband. I had been a little sick when this started, and I was ill with no sleep and stress. So Brenda and I went to see my Doctor for antibiotics and something to help me sleep.*

*To cut down on phone calls, I designated two people I would contact and then asked them to pass the information on to others. A phone tree was good for me, but it was misunderstood by many who thought they were not allowed to call or visit and took it badly.*

*The FBI ladies came and left, and then Edison Chouest came to the house. It was Adrienne, Karen, and Richard. Richard was one of the teams of negotiators from a company that Chouest had used two years ago when C-Endeavour was attacked. He never gave me his business card but said he was from a private firm.*

*I asked my family and friends to leave the house because I felt very vulnerable as they invaded every detail of our lives. Adrienne said she wanted to go over some financial matters with me. I was afraid that she wanted to talk about life insurance. I wanted one piece of our life to remain private. But everyone was there, and I was worried I would cry in front of them.*

*Adrienne and Karen were very friendly and said that Tommy's pay would continue and that they were there if we needed anything. So I asked them to send $1,500 of his pay to my account. I am on Tommy's account, but I didn't have any passwords to pay bills out of his account, and I wasn't even sure which bills had been paid and which ones needed to be paid.*

*Richard talked to me about why his team was there and said they had a lot of experience dealing with these situations. He said this was purely a kidnapping for ransom, and the ship was damaged considerably. I asked Richard all the questions I had asked the FBI and Stephen. I hoped he could give me more information, but he had little. So instead, he told me step by step how he expected this would play out.*

*He stressed the need to stay away from the media and said that the media involvement could only make this turn out badly. He said the exact words that haunted me repeatedly when the FBI said, "Proof of Life." Those were the big deal words they used to say when the kidnappers made contact. We were still waiting for that to happen, and Kathy would only refer to them as "Hostage Takers," never kidnappers, militants, or any of the names I called them.*

*Richard spoke with an accent. He was from Australia and lived in Singapore. He was a fish out of the water at our farm in cornfield, Illinois. Richard explained that sometimes it takes a few days before they would contact the company to ask for ransom and that they felt the kidnappers had reached land by now with the guys. He said there was nothing more that could be done except to wait for the call.*

*I was not in agreement with that. I wanted someone out there to find my husband. NOW!*

*They gave me the chief engineer's wife's telephone number to call her. I asked them if she spoke English because Tommy's regular chief engineer lived in Thailand and had an Asian wife. That was when I learned it was not Tommy's usual chief engineer.*

*After they all left, I was again disappointed and frustrated. I had gotten every cell in my body worked up over this meeting, and poof... nothing happened—no more information.*

*I did call the chief engineer's wife. We compared notes, wondering if one or the other had more information. But we were told the same thing. I felt terrible for her because she did not have a lot of family around her. However, she did say her mother was traveling from out of state to be with her.*

*I went to bed with high hopes of sleep, but this night was the worst so far.*

## Captain Wren Thomas

During our stay, partying, screaming, and smoking crack became the norm. We called it the "1900 hours Party." You could set your watch to it. It was driving me nuts trying to sleep and be awoken to the chaos. After hearing what I called the "Reefer Addict Song" so much, I tried plugging my ears with torn material from one of my t-shirts. That worked about as well as a Gorilla having sex with a Spider Monkey.

It was hard to experience. It was sleep deprivation at its best, and I can only describe it as being the same as how our POWs in Vietnam were treated. The Vietnamese figured out they could torture our men by watching their rapid eye movement (REM). They would see the REM, wake up the prisoner, and then let him fall asleep again. It was torture. We would fall asleep to be awakened to loud music and not only one cell phone, but it was 4 or 5 going simultaneously.

This practice evolved much earlier than in Vietnam. Although the United Nations Convention Against Torture currently bans it, the US permits it. It is referred to as sound disorientation techniques and is utilized as a part of psychological operations as an element in psychological warfare. Blasting loud and offensive music until slowly, the individual's train of thought slows down, and their will is broken. It works because the brain constantly tries to find patterns and make order out of chaos. When presented with something unfamiliar, the brain gets frustrated. Much like my brain would do with the "Reefer Addict Song."

In addition to the cell phones blaring music, they would argue and talk loudly. The only thing I could compare it to would be the craziest Jerry Springer show you have ever seen. It was crazy.

I woke up during the second night at camp and decided I needed to pee, so I started to walk outside when one of the captors chambered a round! I told him what I was doing, and he told me that I must get permission from one of them before leaving our mattress.

Seamar finally got back the next day and told me he couldn't find anything to help my itch but did get two more inhalers (I emptied these into our foam mattress). I did manage to find a bottle of disinfectant called DETTOL. It is their version of Liquid Lysol. I would shower/bath, wash with soap, rinse, and then rub Dettol all over the infected area. I would let it stay there for 15 minutes and then rinse it. I thought for sure, between the antibiotic I was taking twice a day and the Dettol, it would make the infection go away. Of course, it didn't cure it, but it seemed to relieve the pain and itch for a few hours.

Seamar sat and talked to me on our third day outside the

hut. He told me, "Mr. Stone Cold, we knew where you were coming, where you were, and your destination. All we had to do was wait."

Then he said, "We had traveled further offshore than ever."

Well, that explains the reason for being towed by the shrimp boats, as he was lost. However, he said, "I knew where you were as we had arrived at our location just before dark. We saw your lights and knew it was you."

Seamar said, "We started to come to you but decided to wait for you to turn. So when you turned the boat, we were excited because we knew we had you."

He continued, "All I had to do now was wait for you to come to me."

I interjected at that point, "And we did."

Then Seamar said, "Stone Cold, it didn't matter how long you stayed in the citadel. We were not going to leave without you."

Then he said, "You are an American, Mr. Stone Cold, which means you would have gotten hungry soon and come out."

I told him, "You're correct. I am a fat American, and yes, I did get hungry." But then I explained, "You are wrong if you thought you would starve us into submission."

Around the fourth day, HiLo and I figured out about the same time that we had not pooped since leaving the ship, which worried us. The other uncomfortable thing about pooping was having a guard standing there watching you. That sucked. I was used to it being in the Marine Corps and pooping with 30 or 40 other Marines. What they found interesting about us pooping was that we still used hygiene. Without toilet paper, we would use strips of t-shirts I had cut up to wipe our bums with, and they would use their hands.

I had collected some of my shirts we weren't using as pillows and cut them into small strips. We would count our strips to see how many more shits could take before having to start giving up pillow shirts.

While in camp, it was so hot, humid, and miserable that it seemed like the less clothing, the better. Or maybe not. One guy would walk around naked most of the time, holding and rubbing himself, his penis, and his scrotum. This guy would brush his hands across our legs and stare at us while we bathed.

I made the most of my shirts by creating pillows for myself and HiLo, and I started to cut the rest for wiping when we pooped.

We spent the days daydreaming, wondering, thinking, talking, and telling stories. Then, at one point, the pirates started tearing down the weapons to clean them. I quickly learned how reliable an AK-47 is; these things were rusty beyond belief and never jammed or misfired. So they tore them down, scrubbed them, and soaked them in buckets of diesel.

Even as a Marine, we were never allowed to strip our weapons as far down as these men did. Stripping a gun to that level was conducted in the armory. They fired fine. I witnessed this while we were offshore running shrimp boat to shrimp boat.

Every day and every night, anytime they heard a noise, they would chamber a round in their weapons. That sound was scary. We had 14 captors with 5 AK-47s and 1 French-made M-60 7.62 automatic rifle. It was torture at its worst, as we knew that we were dead if this noise was someone trying to rescue us. It was like playing Russian Roulette 24 hours a day. I'm not talking about "let's get drunk and play Russian Roulette," this game was forced.

A million things were going through our heads. First, HiLo and I joked about how it would suck if we got out of here and had to fly coach back to the US. I don't know where that thought came from, but we laughed and joked about it.

The captors offered us cigarettes, and I quit for two months and started again. Shoot, I started back in the speedboat when they took us away from *C-Retriever*. I smoked 3 or 4 a day and saved the rest for my chief, as I had Skoal that I could chew, and I knew he couldn't take Skoal as it made him sick.

During the first few days, a friend of the captors came into camp with his dogs. Come to find out, he was a hunter selling bush meat (a rat) and monkeys. The meat was uncleaned and covered with flies. The fresh (sort of) meat just compounded the number of flies we already had. The shrimp was still lying there over the bamboo cooker. He would stop by now and then.

This man would bring his hunting dogs, usually about 6 of them. It was always a sad time because if the dogs did anything wrong, the Nigerians would kick them or beat them or what freaked me out one time was them grabbing a dog by one of his legs and swinging him around in the air. It was tragic hearing the screams that came from that dog. We had rough nights.

We would sometimes walk in and out of the hut to test our captor's reactions. We listened to our captor's conversations. They would speak in their native language and English. We tried to study our captors – and made mental notes on who had tattoos, what the tattoos looked like, which arm they were on, if there were any words... we studied them hard.

We tried when it was possible to ask about as much of their personal lives as possible. We needed to know as much as possible; as we knew when it was done, we would go through many debriefings.

One of the craziest things I can remember was these crazy Nigerians would always say 'Nanny Boo Boo.' We were like, where in the world did they hear this, and then we figured out it was probably from a TV show. I forget what they told us it meant, but it was something stupid that had nothing to do with the show. It was probably something to do with getting stoned because this is when they said it the most and laughed like idiots.

I got tired and went inside to try to catch some sleep. We were starving and were finally offered a bag of Indomie which are basically like inexpensive ramen noodles. They would cook all the food in pots they had brought and used a fuel burner to heat the pots.

They would dry their fish, shrimp, monkey, bush rat, or

whatever on the bamboo tabletop over the flames. It is best described as a type of open smoker. They would use bottled water when they needed it to cook but would use swamp water to wash the dishes. It was amazing that they were too ignorant to think and collect rainwater.

These swamps were filled with oilfield pollutants, and of course, we were at the bottom of the creeks, which meant we were getting all of the bath water, sewage, and everything else from the villages upstream. Everything includes condoms, tampons, poo, urine, rotten food, animal carcasses, dead bodies, and you name it, I have seen it floating in these rivers and creeks. It was nasty, but what is one to do?

Our health was always on my mind. I would think if it is slack tide when our captors wash the dishes, there is an excellent chance someone just bathed, pissed, or defecated right there where they collected the water. And this was immediate pollution, which could lead to us getting sick immediately.

One of us getting sick was a terrible nightmare. I knew that if one of us got ill, the pirates would shoot us, or we would die. I knew they wouldn't take us to a medical facility, and we didn't have any medicine to care for one of the hundreds of diseases we could have had. They couldn't even find anything to take care of my jungle crotch rot.

With all those thoughts about our health, I pulled out my bag of meds. I took an inventory. I had a big bottle of Doxycycline, two bags of Halls cough drops with vitamin c, a bottle of Tylenol, and a bottle of Advil. I decided it would be best to double the daily dose of Doxy to 1 in the morning and one at night, along with a hall's cough drop each time. We discussed the need to train other Captains to grab some medications to ensure their survival if they are taken from their vessel.

We each ate a bag of this Indomie, which would become our only nutrition. One bag every other day, and none if our negotiator managers pissed off the captors, which was very often.

I continued to have jungle rot. It was bad. It was worse than anything I had ever had. It burned and itched 24 hours a day, with the nights being the worse. After about a week, this started scaring me as the rash traveled down my legs and around my bum. I'm thinking great, infection, and no clinic for miles.

We were both able to defecate. Finally, this was very painful. Besides everything else, I continued worrying about what would happen if one of us became sick. Would we die or what? They didn't want us to die, and I knew this because one day, I scraped the top of my head on the hut's roof, and they were all apologetic. That was also hard to understand. I scrape my head, and they worry. They didn't let us get rest and fed us crap food, and that didn't bother them.

One day as we were eating, all hell broke loose. I think this was day four or five. They had taken one of the Dee, the community boy/ slave, outside the huts. Community Boys/slaves are young men that walk around asking for work. They would hang around the side of the boat at the end of the gangway while we were in, just waiting for us to give them a job. They paint, scrub, clean, carry groceries, and do other jobs. They work for cash when on a boat. They are your neighborhood kid knocking on your door to mow your grass or whatever. Only in Nigeria, these boys can't freely leave. They offer their services in exchange for room and board to survive and are essentially treated as slaves.

They took Dee outside, screaming at him, and the fight was on. They started pushing him, and he shoved back. He was a young kid with a lot of fight in him. Seaman was in town somewhere, so Seamar took charge. They finally got the kid face down on the ground and held him there while the Seamar beat him with a machete blade. I plugged my ears to try and drown out the screaming.

Witnessing this drove me into depression. I couldn't stand to hear the screaming and wondered what pain that poor kid was going through—knowing that it could easily be myself or HiLo being beaten without mercy. But then, when everything calmed down, they let him up.

I buried my face in the foam mattress and sulked because this broke my heart. I was so upset over seeing this. I was hoping that the blade had not injured the kid. I buried my face in my bed while listening to his screams. It broke my heart. I'm not sure why the beating of a community boy affected me so much after what these men did to me, but it did. The only thing I could think of was my fatherly instinct kicking in.

About an hour later, Seamar came back. He talked with the men for a while, saw me, and asked his men what was wrong. Then, knowing I was upset, he grabbed Dee again, made him get on his stomach, and beat him again. Come to find out; the kid had hidden one of the other men's cell phones that the man had stolen off my ship. That was pretty stupid. It's a hard life in the bush for community boys.

It was hard not having contact with the outside world. We didn't know how our crew was coping without us and how the ship was doing. We wondered if our families had found out yet, and how they were coping. We assumed everyone thought we were dead since they had not heard from us in five days.

## Captain Wren Thomas' Son, Dillon Thomas

*During the next few days, there was still no word on whether or not my Father was dead or alive. All I can think of is whether they beat him. Are they feeding him? Is he still alive or not? And, if he is alive, I know he is not sleeping, so how can I sleep?*

## Captain Wren Thomas

On the fifth night, we were awakened and told to grab our things. So we walked down to the pier and boarded the speedboat. It was crazy as hell.

One of our captors had a prosthetic leg and had it along the gunnel of the boat. I couldn't believe it. They said that a boat full of men had shown up the night before offering prawns and fish and that our camp location was compromised.

While waiting in the boat, I told HiLo, "Dude, if shit goes down, I'm rolling out the port side. So you roll out the starboard side and down into the water."

For some reason, our captors changed their minds and decided to wait one or two more nights. So we returned to the hut and tried to go back to sleep, which was impossible as our nerves were done. Seriously, we were at our max stress levels. I could feel my blood pressure rising. Some nights I would look at the roof of the hut and imagine that I was in my bed at home, looking at my wood ceiling, lying next to my wife, with my two dogs fighting for positions. But instead, I listened to the night jungle noises with many types of frogs croaking out to their friends, screeching, buzzing, pulsing, chirping, and trilling. The jungle noises never stop.

Our first week was crazy. The camp was nasty, filled with food waste, urine, and every piece of trash they made spread all over the place. I decided to clean the camp one day, so I walked around picking up all the trash. The captors were bewildered at this. They couldn't understand it. They told me to stop and that they didn't want me getting hurt or sick, but as usual, I told them to get over themselves and continued to do it anyway.

I was given yet another lesson in not trusting a Nigerian. One afternoon Dee asked if I wanted some tea. I told him yes. Then when he got around to it about an hour later, I told him I didn't want it, thinking it wouldn't be good for me to have caffeine.

He went completely nuts and told me never to make him angry again, or I would regret it. He had Satan in his eyes. I apologized to him and accepted some tea.

Between my military training in the Marine Corps and television (TV), I learned to leave markers of my location for anyone coming to help. My marker was empty Skoal cans, as I knew they didn't sell Skoal in Nigeria, and anyone who found them would know we had been there. It was also a military strategy, do not ever throw trash of any sort, as the enemy will know you were there. But in the case of being lost, it is a good idea to leave bits of trash like a popcorn trail.

With Seamar back, we were ordered to call our office on a handheld satellite phone they had stolen off our ship that belonged to our chief officer. We first tried our warehouse manager in Onne. Well, of course, he couldn't hear me. So then we called our office in Port Harcourt. I was forced to tell them a story Seamar made up that HiLo had malaria and was deathly ill.

Lying about that was hard because it had been six days without contact with the outside world. After this call, I was coached to start talking with anger in my voice. It was hard. I had men telling me to talk one way and men telling me to talk other ways. Men told me to tell them we were being poorly treated, and some told me to say we were being treated well.

## Captain Wren Thomas' Wife, Rhonda Thomas

## October 28, 2013

*I got a call from Richard at about 10:00 a.m., telling me that the kidnappers had contacted the office in Nigeria and that they had established proof of life. I asked him what kind of proof of life do you have. He said the negotiators had spoken to him on the phone. Richard stated that Wren and HiLo were uninjured and doing fine. I wanted to know what the negotiator meant when he said Tommy was fine. Richard said they were doing okay, and that's all his information. He said this was precisely how he and his team had suspected it would be. He said that now that negotiations had started, we needed to avoid speaking to the press. Richard said it was very likely that the kidnappers would contact me, attempting to put more pressure on the company to settle for more money or settle faster.*

*According to company policy, he said the crew all hid in the citadel, which is the engine room. He said that the kidnappers cut through the doors with torches and cutting wheels until they could get to the crew. The kidnappers were armed, the two Americans were taken away on another vessel, and the Nigerians were left behind. He said the damage to the ship was so bad it had to be towed to the port. He said that the crew was quarantined until they were all interviewed by authorities.*

*This call was overwhelming because it was good news that "someone" had proof of life, and distressing to hear that my husband sat in an engine room for all that time, getting removed by someone cutting through the door. Brenda had sent me a link she found on G-Captain or another news story, and it said the same thing, but it wasn't confirmed until I heard it from the company. Now it was haunting. Now, this was all I could think about, and I was scared for my husband. It was sickening.*

*The FBI came over that afternoon to tell me the same thing that Richard told me on the phone, almost verbatim. They again said those nasty words, proof of life, and I asked them if I could hear the call. I knew there had to be a recording of it. Or can I see a picture, anything? They said that they would request the company. That evening Dad came over to draw Ruby a picture of a witch on a rocket. My Dad drew an image for me every Halloween for my entire life, and it had become a part of Halloween for me. Ruby wanted to see it too, so Dad came and drew it for her. I went to bed that night and slept some but woke with nightmares about my husband's six hours spent fighting off the kidnappers.*

## Captain Wren Thomas

Storytime went out hunting one night and brought back some monkeys and bushmeat. Neither my chief engineer nor myself knew he was out hunting. All we could hear were gunshots in the distance. That was in itself very frightening.

But when one of their friends was out hunting, that made it 100 times worse. We knew Storytime wasn't out hunting, so we never knew if it was a hunter or the Army or Navy; if it wasn't the Army or Navy, then we were sure that with gunshots going off, someone would soon be snooping in the swamps to find out where the gunshots originated. And again, if we were found, we were dead. We hoped for a rescue, but then again, unless it was 14 SEALs hiding in the bush ready to get off 14 shots simultaneously, maybe biding our time was a better solution.

The monkeys and rats Storytime brought back were disgusting, so we declined them. Thanks, but no thanks. They hadn't been field-dressed, and flies had been nibbling on them all night into the next day. They brought them inside the hut to prepare the monkeys and put them over the fire on a bamboo-created spit. At that point, they would burn all the hair off them. After the burning, they would take them outside, scrape all the burnt hair off, then gut them and wash them in the river (in the same spot where someone defecated, urinated, or bathed), and then bring them in and cook them over the fire.

It was more smoking them than cooking them. I didn't want the fish, monkey, or rat as I knew that if either of us got sick from eating any of this, we would end up probably dead as there was no emergency room in the swamp.

The hut was dirty because they would eat like animals. Seriously, with their bowl of food on the ground, they just slopped food into their mouths with their fingers, sharing bowls with maybe five guys eating at the same time from the same bowl. Then, they would spill food all over the mud floor and leave it, which fed many flies and these silly-looking tadpole-looking creatures. It was like living in a waste dump.

Some nights I would lay there and look at the moon, wondering if my family was looking at the moon at the same time. It seemed like HiLo, and I would tell each other good night five or six times every night. First, we would say good night, then not be able to go to sleep and set up and smoke a cigarette, or I would hit some Skoal. Then, we would repeat good night; every time our captors chambered a round, they would scare us, and we would have to say good night over again.

## Captain Wren Thomas' Son, Dillon Thomas

*On the sixth or seventh day, a little after lunch, I get the call from the FBI "Your Father is alive." Instantly it feels like the weight of another person has been lifted off my shoulders. Still not his condition or situation; I still felt a sense of anger.*

*Why is the only thing they tell me is, "He is Alive." Why are all these people giving information to my Step-Mom, but not me and my brother – his blood?*

*Why are we the last people to find out anything? Why hasn't his company called us to see how we are doing? The worst thing about it was I couldn't go halfway around the world and search for him. All I could do was sit and wait for my phone to ring.*

*I got a call from my cousin, Marshall, on the night we learned he was alive. I stayed in touch with him the whole time my Father was kidnapped. The crazy thing about it is we both pointed out how beautiful the moon was, and we both wondered if my Dad had been doing the same.*

*After praying for the best, I could only start to think about the good times. Like playing hockey in the driveway and Dad breaking the window after fussing at us for breaking one the day before. All the times I see him coming in from offshore, all of the motorcycle*

*club meets, playing with me and my older brother, the metal belt*
*he wore (He never spanked me, but I was scared to death of that*
*belt), teaching us how to be better in sports, the first time he took*
*us ice skating and so on. All I could do was cry.*

## Captain Wren Thomas

We were able to wash what little clothes we had with us. I think
I had one pair of under drawers and cut some jeans to make
shorts. Welcome back to 1970s tacky! I ended up giving HiLo
a pair of nylon shorts and some shirts.

Getting the clothes dry in the heat and humidity was not easy.
Sometimes it would take days if the sun wasn't out, which wasn't
very often as we were heading towards the end of the rainy
season there. I had two pairs of Levi's with me, and I planned
on cutting the legs off both. However, when I asked the pirates
to cut them for me, Seamar overheard my request and freaked
out. He would not allow me to cut the 2nd pair of jeans, as he
wanted me to look nice when we were ransomed.

During the first few calls made back and forth, the ransom offered was 9 million Naira. I didn't have to act angry at this point,
as this made me furious! I knew 9 million Naira ($20,815.51 US
dollars) was close to our Nigerian Fleet's grocery budget for a
month! I was mad as hell! I hated everyone at this point!

HiLo knew this and tried to make me feel better by telling
me, "Well, Mr. Stone, I hate to put it like this, but if there
were anyone I would want to be held captive with, it would
be you."

Well, it sounded stupid, but it worked, we laughed, and I felt
a little stronger.

Several times during the week, I spoke to Seamar and bitched
at him that we were not Nigerians; we were old Americans, and
our bodies and mental health would not last long if things didn't

change. We needed sleep. We needed food. He agreed with me, but nothing changed.

In the first week, I talked to the pirates about my Grandmother, and I told them with a promise that if this killed her, I would be back in Nigeria, and I would bring hell with me. I would also quote *Revelations 6:8, "And I looked, and behold a pale horse: and his name that sat on him was Death, and Hell followed him."*

I would get mad, curse, scream at them, and tell them to read *Rev 6:8*. This was my attitude from the beginning. I didn't take shit from any of them. We talked many times about what we would do if we could take control of the weapons and our captors. We wanted to torture them to death, bring them back to life, and start the torture all over again.

## Captain Wren Thomas' Wife, Rhonda Thomas

## October 29, 2013

*We had an FBI conference call today, and I again asked if I could hear the phone call. I wanted to listen to my husband's voice. I needed my own proof of life. So I got this dude I have never met, spoken to, or even heard of telling me that he has proof of life, and I wanted to listen to it for myself. The FBI said that they made this request and that the company denied it.*

*They said, "Nothing good could come of it" I was furious.*

*At the same time we were all on a conference call, I was texting the FBI ladies asking them to get it for me. One of the ladies, I think Sue said it was the company's property. I texted back that this is supposedly a federal investigation. The federal taxpayers are paying for you to call it your case, so get the tape and let me hear my husband's voice.*

*After that, I got a call from Joe, who was Richard's partner. He* tried to smooth it over and kept changing the subject. Finally, I told Richard that if I were kidnapped, my husband would sit on your desk until I was home, so quit bullshitting me about this.

I didn't believe that they had talked to him. I thought they were only saying all that since it had been so long and no news. I worried I would get bad news very soon, saying, "Oops, we are sorry, guess we messed up."

Joe told me that if the kidnappers called me, do not talk to them. I said but how do I know if it is my husband calling? Sheri and Brenda sat by me as I spoke to him. He said if Tommy calls me, tell him I am sorry I can't talk to you right now and hang up. It was something I could not swallow.

I hung up and told Brenda and Sheri what Joe was asking of me, and I knew that if I answered the phone and it was my husband, there was no way in the world that I could hang up on him. So it's ludicrous that he could even suggest it.

I called back Joe and talked to him again. I quizzed him repeatedly, trying to get him to tell me why he was so convinced that the kidnappers would call me. Instead, he told me several times that he was confident they would attempt to contact me and stressed over and over that if I talked to the kidnappers, it could take months instead of a week or two of negotiations.

He explained that once the kidnappers feel as though they have some other listening ear, they would want more and that they would stop talking to the people on the negotiating team and compromise all the negotiations. He said over and over that this is imperative that we DO NOT speak to them, not even a hello.

That night he called me again from his hotel room and apologized for sounding so harsh. I told him I would think about all this but what he asked of me was more than I should have to do.

## Captain Wren Thomas' Mother, Judy Davis-King

*Meetings and conference calls with the FBI were ongoing daily. Our emotions were all running wild, not on the same page on the same day. When one was angry or down, we would all step in to be there for them. It helped our spirits when we found out the company had proof of life. Thank you, Lord! We were asked not to give their names to the news media or the newspaper for their safety. We were told to monitor all calls and not answer out-of-the-country calls.*

CHAPTER TEN

# Moved to Second Camp

### Second camp 7th day of captivity

### Captain Wren Thomas

Finally, on the seventh day of captivity, the following Wednesday, they woke us up at 3:00 a.m. again. It was almost déjà vu as this was the exact same time I was awoken on my ship the night of the attack.

This time we packed the whole camp and sailed off in three speedboats loaded with everything. We traveled further into the swamps, away from the ocean. After we had sailed for about an hour, we stopped and then slept in the boats in the creeks until daylight came.

While in the creek on our move, we all tried to get comfortable in the boat. I looked at the stars through the tree canopy, smoking cigarettes while my captors smoked their weed. We had the foam mattresses, tools they made, guns, machetes, fishing nets, metal boarding ladders that could hang from gunwales, grapple hooks, everything. The beds were laid across the boats, and some captors found it pleasant to sleep on them. How the boats didn't tip over is beyond me.

It was dark and eerie on the nasty creek, surrounded by thick mangrove trees on both sides, so thick that you could not see if someone or something was hiding there. The mangroves' tops provide a canopy across the creek's top with their leaves. I just knew a snake would drop out of one of the trees.

Storytime told his version of bible stories and explained each sound we heard. You could listen to the monkeys screaming in the distance and, of course, the squirrels. They have a type of squirrel; I guess that's what it is, that makes a loud noise that makes the same sound as a screaming parrot.

When the sun rose and peeked through the tree canopy, we continued up the creek until we found an inland island. This location would become our new home for our remaining days. We arrived at the island, and a few men went ashore to prepare a campsite. We could hear them chopping trees and weeds with machetes. When they had it cleared, one boat with a few men went off to get building supplies, which amounted to more trees. The rest of us went ashore and waited for their return.

We sat and talked while the community boys and a few bushmen gathered bamboo and tore palm leaves into strips to build a new shelter. While we sat and talked and the few workers worked, the remaining few of our captors smoked more weed. I thought just how much weed people could smoke in one day. They were smoking more joints than HiLo, and I were smoking cigarettes. It was baffling and scary as all hell at the same time. Who wants to be with a bunch of stoned men carrying loaded AKs in an already very stressful situation?

The other men finally came back with prepared trees they had cut down and had already chopped the limbs off, so all they had were wooden posts.

They unloaded the boat and began building a shelter. It was amazing how fast the men worked and how well they made a shelter out of nothing but what they found in the swamp. It was about 16 feet long by maybe 12 feet wide and around 6 feet tall, and this was the frame. Then they broke lengths of bamboo in half to make a frame for a pitched roof. After securing the bamboo, they used tarps and covered the top.

After this was accomplished, they built us bed frames. They made two on the East and two on the West, with about a two-foot storage space between the two sides. So now we had four bunks.

But, of course, HiLo and I still were provided with the nasty, moldy, smelly mattress foam about the size of a twin bed. It was much better than sleeping on the muddy ground, but it still sucked. By this point, I had an almost constant migraine from the moldy wet foam. It was our space. I slept lengthwise, and HiLo slept sideways at my feet because he was short. I told him he reminded me of my Labrador, as that is where she would sleep.

We set up our mosquito net for protection, which also sucked because the nets held heat. It was the equivalent of wearing a pair of pantyhose over your entire body. On the other hand, the mosquitoes out here were the size of pterodactyls, so the heat was worth it. The swamp is weird. Unlike different environments, it got hotter after the sun went down. So we were continually hot and sweaty. There was no break in the sticky humidity.

Our captors set up watch posts on each end of the island and one in the front. This island did offer more cover and concealment, should we need to hide during a gunfight. But with a generator running, people screaming, and music blaring, it was still scary with no noise discipline. We spent our days talking and napping. With the captors smoking so much marijuana, we stayed high from all the secondhand smoke. It did make it easier to sleep.

Of course, it seemed like every night was the same. The pirates had their "1900 hours screaming party." Two or three men would go out at night and set gill nets in the river and return the following day to bring in the nets and the catch of fish.

As soon as they returned with their catch, they cleaned them anywhere they could. Sometimes right by the beds, attracting more flies, dumbasses. They couldn't comprehend keeping the food waste away from where they slept.

Then they would cook them up and have fish and garri. Garri is local food and a source of carbohydrates extracted from cassava shrubs' tuberous roots. The cassava root vegetable is poisonous unless you peel it and cook it first. Garri is commonly served in boiled form.

About every third night, a few men would take one of the speed boats and travel to a village nearby to purchase more marijuana, cigarettes, soap, body lotion, and hair cream. On one particular night, two or three pirates had left to get a resupply of weed, cigarettes, soap, etc., and didn't show back up in the expected amount of time given to them by their leader Seamar. I want to say it was around 9:00-10:00 p.m.

We had been asleep but were rapidly awoken by the sound of the men locking and loading their weapons. HiLo and I were curious about what was going on. We found Dee and asked him what was going on. He told us that the men that went out were still not back and that a few men would find and kill them.

I guess it was after midnight when they all returned. Again, the pirates had to lock and load their weapons. It was always a bitch to wake up to that sound. It's one alarm clock I will never forget. They drug the two men up the bank. The men were thrown on the ground right by the reefer addicts' bunk and made them lie face down in the mud.

Seamar was pissed and very excited. When Seamar got pissed or excited, he would scream, stutter and start blending his native and English; when he shouted, he was loud. Once again, no noise discipline. The two men on the ground had guns pointed at them, with Seamar standing over them about to beat the living shit out of them with a machete when they finally cried enough and talked him into listening to them about what happened.

I forget the excuse, but I remember that they were all hugged up with some village girls when they were located. They had been drinking and then had sex and fell asleep.

I didn't like either one of these dipshits. I was hoping that Seamar would beat the shit out of them with the sharp end of the blade instead of beating them with the side of the blade as he did to Dee. These dickheads didn't even deserve a bullet. The longer we were there, the harder it was to deal with them. Which also made it harder to go to sleep and remain asleep. On top of that, we still had problems defecating as it would only come about once every three or four days.

The nights were getting hotter, and the thunderstorms were coming more frequently, lightning striking all around. Finally, after around 02:00 a.m., all but maybe one man would be asleep, and sure as anything, that man couldn't stand it and would come up talking to himself or playing on his cell phone as loud as possible. It would wake me every time; when others awoke, it was impossible to sleep.

I still don't understand why I took care of Dee so much, but I guess I was like a father to him. On one particularly stormy night, he asked if he could crawl in the bed with my engineer and me. As much as I wanted to say no, I just couldn't. It was as if I felt sorry for him.

Dee didn't belong there. His mother had just passed at the beginning of the year, and his beloved sister was off to college in Calabar (the capital of Cross River State, Nigeria). We talked a lot.

We asked him why he was there, and he didn't have an answer besides he was good friends with Seamar. So we asked him if he knew what he was getting himself into, and Dee said he had no idea. Dee then stated that what he did know was he was never coming back and never doing anything like this ever again.

After about a week, I finally got Dee to stop sagging, which was a significant accomplishment since I still couldn't get my youngest son to stop. Dee was a good boy.

## Captain Wren Thomas' Sister, Brenda Wright-Rockamann

*Frustrations were building as my brother's sons did not feel they were getting the same news, attention, and focus in Louisiana that we were getting here on the home front. My brother had two sons and two grandsons at the time. They are very close to their mother, who was still a close friend to my brother. They were married for almost twenty years, yet no information could be given to her by authorities to help her support or comfort her children because they were no longer married. So it made it very hard on the boys.*

*They were turned away by their father's employer when they drove there seeking answers. Their hearts were breaking. We tried our best to keep them informed daily, but there was not much to tell most days.*

*Blake and Dillion live near the headquarters of Edison Chouest. In their local community, the kidnapping was a significant news event resulting in a lot of media coverage. It was the hot topic for conversation across the town, too. There were all sorts of rumors and embellishments to some of the stories. The boys would hear stories and be hurt, thinking that information had been withheld from them. Yet, I was constantly going to bat for them making sure that they were not forgotten by anyone, as did their stepmother Rhonda.*

## Captain Wren Thomas' Son, Dillon Thomas

*A few days go by, and still no new words from the FBI. At this point, I am angry and frustrated about everything. His company never tried to reach out to my brother or me. A simple call would have been fine. The FBI offered to include me in the conference call, but I refused. I got tired of hearing the same thing every day "We're sorry, over and over." I am like, don't be sorry, get my DAD.*

*I want to say day ten is when we got the call that they spoke to him and he is alive. That was an enormous weight off my shoulders, but I was still angry, and my Dad wasn't back home yet.*

*The Media started getting crazy, calling my boss, old landlords, friends' houses, Facebook, you name it. It seemed these people only wanted a story and could care less about my Dad.*

## Captain Wren Thomas

One day I needed a Bible very desperately. I wanted to read *Revelations* as I knew time was coming to an end, and I wanted to make sure I understood how it would play out.

Other times I thought of ways to torture our captors that would make the Devil cringe. I believe God would have had to come up with a new place to send me as I would have put them thru so much misery and torment that the Devil would have been scared to let me in hell. I often thought of doing this to some of my managers, especially those who set us up upon our return.

We were both incredibly pissed and hated everyone. Some crazy stuff goes through your mind when you're in this situation, and to make it worse. We did not know how the situation would unfold on the office side.

There were times when I would just go off. I would scream at our captors and curse at them. One day after they got off the phone with our Nigerian area manager, they were pissed. They were talking in their native language, but in the middle of the conversation, they had said something in English about killing someone.

At that, I was gone. I jumped up and got right up in Seaman and Seamar's faces, screaming at them, "Who will you kill? Are you going to kill us? If you want to kill us, walk down to the creek with me and pull the trigger!" I continued screaming, "It would be my honor to meet God before you."

Well, of course, they didn't do it, but it took a long time for them to calm me down.

I would spend my days walking around the camp to get exercise and fight boredom. I cleaned the second camp twice. First, I would walk around picking up all the trash. They still couldn't understand why I would do that. I also continued to drop markers, my empty Skoal cans, like a popcorn trail to show where I was held.

One day I walked to the end of the island and watched as the captors swapped out engines on the speedboats. It looked too much like work, and I was like, forget about it. I am tired of helping the enemy. So I sat there, smoked a cigarette or two, chewed a little Skoal, and laughed at them. When HiLo came to see what was going on, we both laughed.

## Captain Wren Thomas' Wife, Rhonda Thomas

## November 2, 2013

*Ruby was supposed to go to her Dads this weekend, but at about 8:00 p.m. on November 1, 2013, he called, and she was crying to come home. He was ok with it if I wanted her home. She was sobbing, afraid they would find Tommy if she left home for the night. She didn't want to miss anything, and we thought she might just want to be home to take care of me. When she got home, I bathed her and explained that this whole thing might take a very long time, and she couldn't stay home without going to her Dads.*

*I agreed to let her take her iPad to her Dad's this weekend so she could facetime me, which turned out to be a mistake because she did it all the time.*

*They all left in the afternoon, and we were alone in the house for the first time since day one. Ruby was gone, and finally, I could unload. I went to my room, lay in bed, and sobbed for hours.*

*Eventually, I fell asleep for some time, and Brenda came to check on me later.*

## Captain Wren Thomas

I always prayed for rain. I needed it but didn't need it. So when it would rain heavily, I would grab a bar of soap and take a nice fresh shower. Then, I would stand out in the rain, get muddy, and wash it off.

I loved to freak out and piss off my captors. So knowing they believed in 'JooJoo,' I would go out to where we would shower in the second camp and rub mud all over me. Sometimes I would just paint marks similar to Indian tribal patterns on my face with the mud. Then I would sit in a trance-like state just to freak them out.

I knew how to mess with them and tried to do it as much as possible. I wanted our captors to know they kidnapped the wrong American.

Plus, I had plenty of time to do stupid shit to pass the time. Sometimes I would stay out in the rain, even with thunder and lightning, for so long that Seamar would get pissed and make me come back inside the shelter. I loved being out in the rain and enjoying clean water. It was either this or bathe in the creek's nasty, contaminated swamp water.

Seamar didn't want either of us to get hurt or sick. It struck me as odd, so I asked him about this one day. He told me the one thing they didn't want was for the US to get pissed at them (Nigeria) because he knew that if anything did happen, well, as I said, *Revelations 6:8.*

It was probably inside the second week that Seamar and Seaman were getting angry. Angry to the point of scary. They finally had a big plan for me to tell my manager that I got shot in the leg and was dying and that my engineer was almost dead from malaria. Well, that didn't work. I am just glad it was a bluff and not the real thing.

The captors and I tried everything. They had begun to get nasty, and I believe they threatened the negotiators that they would kill us. It was hard to understand at times what they were discussing.

During some of the calls towards the end, they would chamber rounds in their weapons close to the phone. I guess in an attempt to get the negotiating team to believe that we would get shot. But, of course, all we could figure out was that the Nigerian manager wasn't telling our senior managers everything and that he didn't give a shit if we got killed or not because he helped set us up. Again not knowing how it all works sucked.

And at this point, I screamed at Seamar, "Just kill me! Shoot me in the head and get it over with."

I told him, "At least my misery would be over, and my family would be rich after collecting my huge life insurance policy."

Here was when I knew he was too weak to pull the trigger. My manager quit speaking to me. I was getting very nasty on the phone with him. After about a week at the first camp, we were all getting pissed at our Nigerian manager as things were just not going as quickly as they should.

I talked Seamar into taking HiLo up the river until they got cell phone range so he could speak to our office in the US. I also wanted him to call my wife. I knew I couldn't talk to my wife, and HiLo knew he couldn't speak to his.

They left right after dark and didn't come back until well after 10:00 p.m. HiLo came back looking like he had seen a ghost. He had talked to our Assistant manager in the US and said that the manager was not pleased with our Nigerian manager, which gave me hope. But, unfortunately, he didn't get to talk to my wife, as she wouldn't answer her phone. That sucked, but I figured she was at work and couldn't answer.

Our US assistant manager asked us to call back the next

night. HiLo didn't want to do it but did it anyway. So they left about the same time the next night and got back about the same time, and again HiLo looked as if he had seen a ghost.

I asked him why he said, "Mr. Stone, you don't understand." I said, "Like what?"

He said, "That was the scariest shit I have ever experienced. Every boat that came by or we passed, I was scared it was the Nigerian Navy, and I would die."

After more small talk to calm him down, we finally fell asleep in a pool of sweat.

## Captain Wren Thomas' Wife, Rhonda Thomas

## November 3, 2013

*When I woke in the morning, I was entirely rested and felt like it was time to get life as usual again as possible. I wanted Brenda to do the same. She was a lifesaver all this time, but I couldn't stop wondering when it would be her turn to unload, just as I had the day before. I felt like my mind prevented me from resting or unloading all that because I had Ruby every day, and until she was gone, I couldn't cry.*

*Brenda didn't want to go home; she wanted to stay, but all I could think of was all the things Brenda was talking about doing at home and feeling as though I was preventing her from it. So I made her go, and it sucked bad.*

*Uncle Denny came that morning just as Brenda left, and I asked him to go home too. He had been there every day, and it was time for me to take care of myself.*

*I cried after everyone left and went to the barn to work with the horses. I spent hours in the barn and barely made it in the house for the dreaded 4:30 FBI conference call. I was sick of talking to them. I was sick of every time Brenda said anything to them about*

*MEND or other things we had read about; they would chastise us and make it sound like we were stupid. I am not college educated, but I feel like many of the things they told us were condescending.*

*I can't remember who else was on the conference call that day. I can't even admit whether or not I was listening to any of it, it just felt like a chore that needed to be done, and I was tired.*

*I went to Champaign that night to pick up Ruby, and we stopped to see my Dad for a few minutes and went home to get ready for bed.*

*I went to bed that night and was very angry. My husband was supposed to be home by the weekend, and this is Sunday night, and he still isn't home, so this was bullshit. I was starting to feel like HiLo's wife and wanted to drive to Louisiana, but I didn't have enough money to get there.*

## November 4, 2013

*I went to work at the high school today. It was Monday morning, so I knew I would hear from the company and the FBI again. It was getting to be a pattern to hear lots on Mondays and nothing on weekends. It sucked because it felt like business as usual to them, but this was not normal to us.*

*Joe called a few times throughout the day and strongly warned me that the kidnappers had stopped talking to the negotiating team. They weren't getting what they wanted, and it had been long since they spoke. Nevertheless, Joe was sure that the kidnappers would call me.*

*At 12:30 p.m., 12:31 p.m., and 12:45 p.m., I got calls from Nigeria. I was at work and looked at the phone to see the number and nearly had a heart attack.*

*I was shocked and hurt and wanted to answer the phone badly. I wanted to talk to my husband.*

*It rang over and over in my head that answering the phone could delay this badly. Not answering was forcing the kidnappers to talk to the negotiating team.*

*I was so upset I had to leave work. I told nobody about it. I just called Joe and called Kathy from the FBI and told her.*

*I wanted to warn Judy, Sheri, and Brenda because they should be prepared to get them, too, but I decided that they had already been warned plenty about it, and it was best not to share this more trauma with them.*

*That was probably the hardest thing I ever did in my life. I cried for hours, wondering if this might have been my last chance to hear my husband's voice. I was furious.*

*That evening the FBI came to the house instead of a conference call. We got the rest of the family on the phone to tell them about stalled negotiations, but I asked them not to tell anyone about the calls yet. Time passed, and we were all dragging down and tired, and this was more than I wanted to share.*

*It wasn't for a few days that I went to Brenda's house and told her I got the calls. It was another sleepless night.*

## Captain Wren Thomas

Seamar was a weird son of a bitch. He didn't feed us anything but Indomie (ramen noodles) every other day, and when negotiations went poorly, we wouldn't eat at all. But, he worried about me catching a cold.

During the last week of our captivity, I was very over being there and decided to spruce up my area, so I gathered some small branches with leaves, some palms, and sticks and made them like a small flower garden. I had surrounded it with tree bark and rotten wood pieces, and then I crumbled some of the rotten wood and spread it over my garden as mulch.

It wasn't much, but it gave me something to do and some beauty to look at for the rest of my stay. The other standout was the iguana, the other lizards, some squirrels, and a few birds.

I did have a friend to keep me company. HiLo was lucky as

he had two. Ok, our friends were these little sideways walking land crabs. I named my crab Wilson after Tom Hanks volleyball he had in the movie *"Castaway,"* and also after my brother-in-law Mr. Wilson. HiLo named his two crabs Walker and Texas Ranger. They were not much, but they did occupy our time. HiLo would throw his cigarette butts to his buddies, and I would throw old Skoal to mine. We would both throw them scraps of food.

One night, I got so beyond pissed off that I wanted to kill this pirate. The reefer heads were, of course, smoking their reefer when one of them saw Wilson and threw an empty glass bottle at him. I thought I saw Wilson raise his claw before he ran into his hole. But I figure he gave the reefer head the finger, laughed, and said, "Screw you, your stoned ass missed me."

Our crab buddies were lots of fun. They were skittish, but they seemed to get used to us. We would lie on our beds and watch them for hours. To eat, they would take a piece of bamboo in one claw, peel off a strip with the other, and then hold it up to their mouth. They were pretty cool.

Our other enjoyment was watching what looked like an iguana. The iguana would very carefully slink inside the camp and try to steal food. After a day or two, he finally found the prawns that the Pirates still had over the smoker cooker. It seemed like two or three times a day; he would use his stretched-out fingers and toes with sharp nails to climb up the bamboo legs on the cooker and steal some prawns. I don't even know how he was eating them. Those prawns had to be insanely nasty as they were two weeks old, setting out covered with flies, and where there are flies, there is fly poopoo.

I started to realize just how interdependent HiLo and myself had gotten. I awoke one night and couldn't feel him at my feet. I called his name, and he wouldn't answer. Scared, I started to scream his name.

He yelled back, "Mr. Stone, I am over here."

He was down the path with one of our captors.

It scared the living shit out of me. I thought HiLo was gone. HiLo and I learned after a while that unless someone came to rescue us, we would make it out of there alive. Our twisted version of Stockholm Syndrome.

We both would go off on our captors. We were done with them and their nasty ways. I was a bit worse than HiLo because of my temper. I repeatedly told them, "You kidnapped the wrong American."

I begged them to shoot me every day. I pushed their buttons regularly, trying to make them shoot me.

I remember one particular time I thought HiLo was going to bust a vein in his neck, we both had our days, and this was his. He was beyond sick and tired of all of the bullshit. He stood up and went completely off on the captors.

He told them, "How could you capture Americans? As much as America does for Nigeria? If it weren't for ex-pats, Nigeria would be worse off than it already is."

He continued about how none of them would have a job without Americans. His fury surprised me. The Biker finally came out of him.

I would always ask them, "Why do you always hit my companies' ships? We hire more Nigerians per ship than any other shipping company in Nigeria."

They answered that American companies pay the ransom.

We were at our second location maybe a week when we noticed that a few men were gathering bamboo one day. So we again were like, what now. They were building little tables and placed four of them around the camp.

They placed a pack of Indomie (ramen noodles), garri, a bottle of gin, and fruit on each one. After this, Preacher went to each site and did about forty-five minutes of chanting in a tongue dialect.

Wondering what this meant, I asked one of the leaders and

learned that they did this because they knew the Bush Gods were angry with them.

I said, "Well, all you do is pollute the bush. Why don't you try to take care of it instead of destroying it?" Well, that was too much for them to understand.

One of the funniest things that happened was probably in the second week. HiLo was lying on his stomach on our foam mattress while talking. He had his butt pointing north, and right beside his butt was Preacher's face. How Preacher was so stupid to put his head directly by HiLo's butt was beyond me. Well, I am sure you can tell where this is going... Suddenly, HiLo let out the loudest fart I have ever heard. It was long, and it was loud. It scared the living shit out of Preacher. Preacher was disgusted. Farting in Nigeria is a big no-no and is considered very disrespectful.

Well, I tried not to laugh but choked, holding it back. When I heard some of the Nigerians start laughing, that made it even funnier. We were all laughing for a good while. For some reason, gas is always amusing.

Preacher decided it was time to go to the other end of the island and light up some crack.

HiLo one day says, "Hey, Mr. Stone, why in the hell do you get up and go piss so much?"

I told him, "Hey, shithead, can you think of anything else for me to do? I want to be away from here."

Well, we both laughed. We would find the most stupid shit to do and talk about ridiculous shit just to pass the time.

You have to understand about 90% of all seaman are really immature, "When I grow up, I want to be a Toys "R" Us kid." well, that's me. Two things will sink a ship. One is fire. The other is boredom. My ship is usually far from boring. It is sometimes stressful but never dull. In a time of so much stress, I think laughing and trying to have some fun keeps you sane.

There was nothing fun about our situation, and don't let me mislead you. It was horrible, stressful, scary as anything, and on top of it, depression, anger, sadness, and more stress that came with being the Captain and knowing I had just given up my ship.

I was always worried about being shot, but after that, I stressed over what I did wrong and what I could have done differently, so none of this would have ever happened. I thought about training other merchant mariners to avoid hijackings and survive a kidnapping for ransom. I think I must use the time here to help ensure others don't end up here.

Those thoughts would haunt me at any time or any day. It was also challenging to think that you could die from someone trying to rescue you or die when one of the captors gets high and starts shooting you, or anyone of them shooting us because the Bush Gods told them. One of the concerning thoughts was us getting hit in the crossfire by our captors during one of their many intense arguments.

Being the lucky one, I had just gone to my Doctor and got prescribed Wellbutrin (an anti-depressant) to help me quit smoking. Now I was taking it to deal with the stress of being captive in Nigeria. Lucky for me, I fought hard enough with Seamar that he let me get them before we left the vessel.

HiLo and I could tell when the other was getting depressed, and we would do everything we could to cheer each other up. A really good fart usually did the trick, or we would make fun of one of our captors.

One of the things I told HiLo was just to remember, my brother, that many of our fellow Americans have been through worse. I was referring to all of the POWs in our wars. I have read about the Vietnam War and the Bataan Death March in the Philippines during WWII.

I prayed, and I mean, I prayed a lot. I usually prayed for my Captors. I prayed for God to protect them and asked him to please watch over them, and last but not least, our family and friends.

I had to pray. I knew and could feel millions of prayers every day. I especially felt my Mother's and Grandmother's prayers. I knew God was listening, and this was one of God's trials. I felt God was telling me he did this for a reason and that I would hear his explanation soon.

It was a very dark night between midnight and 3:00 a.m. when one of our captors woke me up by tapping my head with the barrel of his rifle. I turned and looked up at the barrel of an AK, and one of the Pirates was holding it. He bent down and whispered for me to go with him. HiLo was out dead asleep.

Not knowing what he wanted, I followed the pirate in the pitch-black dark of night. The moon was hidden in the clouds, as were the stars. I followed him to the western side of the camp, where we were well hidden by everyone else. We were concealed by the walking legs of mangrove trees, palm fronds, and other weeds and trees. It was quiet in the night except for the occasional screaming of the monkeys or the screaming of the squirrels.

Once we were there, secluded in the foliage growing around, where no one could possibly see us, he told me in a very ominous tone that he 'wanted some of me.' He was deadly serious with a rifle shoved point-blank on my head. He then said that he would shoot me if I screamed or said a word. Then he said he would explain to his leaders that he found me trying to escape if I did not comply.

This filthy fucking animal then proceeded to rape me. It was so incredibly beyond painful. At that point, I would have preferred to be dead. It took everything I had to scream. It took everything I had in me not to fight, not to kill the fucker right then and there. It took everything in me not to give up on life right then and there and force him to shoot me. I cannot imagine any worse torturous act that could be perpetrated against a man. This total subjugation by him was humiliating.

Through everything that had happened, this was by far the worst. I'm not homophobic, but that bastard was a filthy, nasty animal. He was such a repulsive excuse for a human being.

Following this brutality was a very tough period; it was my darkest hour and the most challenging time to keep my faith in God.

I found it hard to believe this happened because we had been trained that homosexuality is not legal in Nigeria. They have laws that law forbids same-sex sexual partners. Punishments are severe, ranging from 10 to 14 years in prison.

I feel this animal stole part of my soul more than the kidnapping. I couldn't bring myself to tell anyone as I knew the FBI already had their hands tied in Nigeria. I knew the Nigerian Government wasn't going to do anything about the whole thing, so why put myself through more humiliation by giving this part? I couldn't do it.

This subjugation is now most of my nightmares, the absolute horrors of that night. I initially did not tell anyone. Not even HiLo. Not the FBI nor my office, Doctors, Psychiatrist, no one. After building trust, I finally told my attorney. But this filthy animal's disgusting, torturous acts cannot go unanswered.

It was probably somewhere around the 3rd or 4th of November when our captors were watching their gathering, or what I will call a club party. We had recognized the chant they had been saying, and a couple of hundred militants were in attendance.

I guess it was a gathering. Those in attendance started talking, then screaming about the jobs (crimes they had committed). It was an extensive range of crimes, from stealing to kidnapping, and it almost turned into a brawl about who was lying and who did the most messed up shit. They talked about bank robberies, the people they had killed during kidnappings, Army, Navy, and Police Officers they had killed during crimes. It was a brag session trying to figure out who was the biggest criminal. But, on the other hand, it was something I didn't want to hear.

If they weren't lying, these pirates were accustomed to killing and probably wouldn't think twice about killing us if necessary. But then, they started talking about their future plans. They planned first to find our Nigerian manager, whom they were negotiating with, kill him and his family, and threaten to wipe out his village. They were serious about this, as they hated him more than anything.

One part of the group decided they would do some bank robberies around Bayelsa State in November, and then come December, they were going to attack another Ship. They were open about past and future plans.

Around day thirteen, we started getting excited. We thought this wouldn't last more than fourteen days from the beginning.

We were saddened and angry that we were still doing negotiations on the fourteenth day. I guess the next men that get kidnapped can expect eighteen days. Our figure came from when the *C-Endeavour* was attacked. The two Americans and one Mexican were held for fourteen days.

During our last week, our captors finally learned from me about collecting rainwater. I would take an empty bucket, fill it with rainwater, and then bathe. So when they finally figured it out, they started using a big plastic trash can and would use this water for cooking and cleaning the dishes.

How much good it did them to collect rainwater, I don't know because they would set their dog food bowl in the mud and eat with four or five men eating out of the same bowl. I would make sure at night to piss all over where they would typically lay their dog bowl.

*Photos included capturing Wren Thomas's journey, with the year noted when available. All other photos are labeled "After" for images captured after Wren's captivity and "Before" to designate images before his life-changing kidnapping.*

C-Retriever, the supply vessel Captain Wren Thomas was kidnapped from off the coast of Nigeria by pirates. The 15-yr-old ship at the time was 240 feet long and more than 2092 tons, operated by Chevron to support the Agbami oil field. Wren took this photo while waiting on a helicopter on a drilling rig just days before he was kidnapped. (BEFORE)

Captain Wren Thomas standing outside of the ship bridge on the M/V DEEP STIM, a well stimulation vessel contracted to Schlumberger, an oilfield services company. (BEFORE)

Wren in 2011 on his 2006 Harley Davidson Road King. This image was taken before his kidnapping, at a time when wishes didn't include having ransom paid, being freed, and staying alive. (BEFORE)

Pensive, with the weight of leading a ship in international waters, this picture was taken of Captain Thomas working on ship paperwork in his thirties. (BEFORE)

Christmas photo of Rhonda Thomas, daughter
Ruby, and Wren Thomas, taken a year before their
world completely changed. (BEFORE)

Towering at 6'2", Captain Thomas on
the bridge of a ship in India. (BEFORE)

Wren Thomas, pirate survivor, flying home
in November 2013 from Galliano, Louisiana,
to Champaign, Illinois. (AFTER)

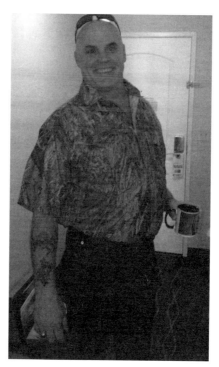

Finally, a good shower, shave, and new
clean clothes. Wren Thomas the day
he flew from Nigeria into Galliano,
Louisiana. His eyes revealed the happiness
of being back in the United States and
out of captivity. (November 2013)

Wren Thomas (AFTER)

Beaux, Wren's beloved service dog, helped
him survive his PTSD from 2015–2019
until his devastating loss. (2015)

Wren Thomas and Beaux taking a break from
service dog handler training at Tackett Service
Dogs in Orange County, California. (2015)

Wren & Beaux, Christmas 2015.

Thanksgiving the year before being taken hostage. From left
to right - sister (Brenda Wright Rockamann), sister (Sheri
Thomas Wilson), Wren, sister (Kari Richards Tiffey), grandma
(Geneva Davis), mom (Judy Davis King). (2012)

Wren Thomas (2012)

Wren Thomas with his adult sons the year before pirates overwhelmed his ship. From left to right - oldest son (Blake Wren Thomas), Wren, youngest son (Dillon Ray Thomas). (Louisiana 2012)

Wren Thomas's United States Marine Corps boot camp photo. (1989)

Wren Thomas's tattoo completed in Champaign, Illinois, after his release from captivity. He always wanted to remember that he survived. (After)

Wren Thomas with his siblings and mother. From left to right - Brenda, Wren (Tommy), Judy, Sheri, and Kari. (After)

## CHAPTER ELEVEN

# The Negotiations

## November 8, 2013

November 8, and things were down to the wire, and the situation was incredibly tense. Our area manager and Seaman had been calling back and forth many times today, and things on both ends were not good. The negotiations were not going well and not progressing fast enough for our captors or us. Worst of all, Seaman, the twelve-year-old-boy-looking second in command, was getting pissed. Seaman is psycho. Seriously, he was not all there and was unpredictable. At the same time, Seaman kissed Seamar's butt and would do anything to ensure he impressed him.

Finally, sometime in the afternoon, an agreement was made. The negotiators went about 5,000 Naira ($11.66 U.S. Dollars) over what the captors would take to release us. It made us happy. It was insane. The captors were cheering and slapping us on the back, telling us we were going home! We knew we were going home! I immediately returned to the hut, sat down on that moldy foam mattress, and started sorting what I would take with me and what was trash. I was putting the good stuff into a backpack I had acquired somehow. I was ready to go, NOW.

Shortly after Seaman got off the phone with our manager and

the cheering calmed down, Seaman and Seamar took HiLo and me to the side and told us how it would play out. First, they would go to Brass and collect the ransom, and then they, and one of our agents, would come back with a boat that was covered for our protection (our protection, this didn't make sense, I will tell you later how it became to make sense). So we were cool with this. After all, we were going home.

Seaman and Seamar left to do the dirty deed at around 3:00 p.m. We all expected them back within a couple of hours. Waiting on this was like waiting for Christmas morning. Waiting for your sixteenth birthday, knowing your dad would get you a brand new Camaro. Or your virgin girlfriend telling you she would give you some December 19, and today is December 18. We were excited.

I think Dee gave us little extra noodles that night in celebration. Our captors were celebrating as much as we were. They were sick of being in the swamp themselves. Then, along came the "1900 hours. Party." They would not miss this for anything in the world.

Then as time passed, it was 8:00 p.m., and then 9:00 p.m. came and went. By 10:00 p.m., everyone at the camp was tripping out.

HiLo and I dosed on and off, and an argument awakened us. We were immediately concerned. What was going on? We soon found out, and we did not like what we heard. Seaman and Seamar still weren't back. So the four or five men started believing that Seaman and Seamar had gotten the ransom money and left. It made sense, a lot of sense.

But it also sucked. So ok, Seaman and Seamar stole the money from the team. So now it was time to start wondering what would happen to HiLo and me. Well, we could see only three possible choices; #1 They would kill us. After all, why keep us alive? They had no ransom money and no more money for food, water, crack, pot, and diesel fuel for the generator that charged their cell phone so they could torture us with the chaotic noise. #2 They could take us to a local village and say they rescued us. #3 They would keep us out there until they were paid again.

Option #3 was out of the question because they didn't have money for food or water. So I would not drink any river water.

The whole night was incredibly stressful. The two leaders had the satellite phone with them, so there was no way to contact anyone. The excitement from earlier was crashing down, so everyone was devastated.

I couldn't sleep that night. Options kept running through my mind. What is going to happen now? We needed a plan. I finally got pissed off and crawled out of bed around 05:00 a.m. on November 9, 2013. I woke up because one of the captors was lonely and decided that he needed to blare his music right by us. It was pretty standard by now, and I was ready to sleep at home, in my bed.

I waited impatiently for everyone else to wake up. HiLo woke up right after me. Looking around, I noticed a couple of rifles quickly within our reach. That is when we started to debate. HiLo and I thought about the fact that we did not know about these rifles. Should we go for the guns or not? We decided not.

With our luck, we would mess up trying to shoot someone, as AKs are way different from ARs, and I had never had training with an AK. Even watching these guys do it all day long, I still couldn't figure out how they were chambering rounds and taking them off safety. We also knew that without a shadow of a doubt, if we killed every one of these no-good sons of bitches in the camp, we would likely get found guilty of murder and hanged. That's just the way things go in Nigeria.

I got with Preacher and Storytime at around 9:00 a.m. when they were up. I bitched, cussed, and screamed until they listened to me. (They told me one night that I was a pain in the ass cause I always bitched; well, forget you is what I said to them.) I told these two geniuses that what needed to happen was they should send a couple of the more intelligent men up the river until they were able to get cell phone reception to call Seaman or Seamar and ask them what was going on.

After arguing, they reluctantly agreed and sent two men up the river to make the call. They probably only agreed to shut me up, but who cares? They went.

The next part of the day sucked. It took them a few hours to get there and back. Meanwhile, we were all sitting on pins and needles, not knowing what was happening and what would happen. Everyone at the camp was stressed. We were so happy to be going home yesterday, so returning to sitting and waiting was even harder than before. HiLo and I just tried to stay quiet and out of the way.

When the men Preacher and Storytime had sent up the creek returned to the island, they told us they had talked to Seaman. They reported that Seamar and Seaman ended up staying in a village overnight because the negotiators were not cooperating as they should. The negotiators wanted to do a hand-to-hand exchange. The rescuers get us, and the captors get the ransom. They said we should expect the Seamar and Seaman back at camp soon.

Well, "soon" turned out to be 4:30 p.m., which sucked. During the time between the two men returning with the news and the time when Seamar and Seaman returned, we all started worrying. It was tense.

Their version of "soon" was too long, and we now thought Seamar and Seaman pulled the bullshit card. So I started gathering empty water bottles to collect rainwater as we were down to two or three bottles. I was sucking down one and a half (or more) each day, which didn't include what HiLo drank.

CHAPTER TWELVE

# The Turn Over

## November 9, 2013

I was nervous and even more scared when we finally heard the sound of a boat engine. Being accustomed to the sounds of the different engines, the remaining captors knew it was Seaman and Seamar. When they arrived, all hell broke loose. They were pissed, and the rest of the captors were excited and happy. Then, again, the slaps on the back started. Dee hugged both of us, telling us he loved us and would miss us very much.

The leaders took us off to the side and called the "Headman," who would deliver the ransom money and collect us. He talked to HiLo and me to ensure we were alive and assured us it would all be over soon. Well, I was like, good, I certainly hope so. But, Seamar told us we would leave just before dark, so we waited.

As we waited, all the captors that were going to travel with us put on their war faces. They tied rags around their heads and wrists because they thought this was cool and intimidating. I thought it was stupid, but that's my opinion. Once they got their war game going on, each one stood in front of Preacher to get blessed, and with the blessing, they had gin thrown on them.

Many locals in Nigeria feel that with the proper JooJoo, bullets will go through them without hurting them, or bullets will go around them, kind of the Superman effect. They are so uneducated that it's bizarre. It's not just this particular group of Nigerians, either.

I told HiLo about a time before the kidnapping when I was on the bridge one day talking to my regular chief engineer about our country's defense system. My Nigerian mate, who is the guy who threatened me over the phone, butts in and says that Nigeria's defense system far surpasses the United States. We were like ok, explain this one to us.

He says a friend of his in the Army told him that the President of Nigeria had strategically placed giant magnets around the country. If war broke out, he would turn on these magnets that would pull in any missiles or fighter planes that flew into Nigeria's airspace. We laughed until we hurt ourselves. My mate didn't think it was funny as this was the truth. HiLo and I got a good laugh out of that story to ease the tensions.

Dusk was approaching fast, so Seamar decided they had been 'JooJooed' about as much as eight men could be 'JooJooed,' and we loaded up. It was surreal to be reboarding the same old, worn speedboat they took us from our ship to be released. With one of the pirates driving the boat, I sat on the next bench forward, and HiLo sat in front of me with a guard on each side of us and one guard at the bow.

We were about 30 minutes into the creek when we came to a junction that led off in about five directions and stopped. At this time, Preacher, who was at the helm, stood up and started his 'JooJoo' chant again but included HiLo and me in the gin part. This chanting went on for about 30 minutes, and then we all were showered with gin, thanks to Preacher. So now we are underway again, praying to God that this will be over soon.

We pounded in the river for about 15 minutes when Seamar decided it would be better to put my fat ass up in the bow and moved HiLo right behind me. So now I am uncomfortable lying on ropes with the point of one of their grapple hooks jabbing me in the side. I tried to adjust, and Seamar screamed at me to stay down.

The trip was stressful; every boat we passed meant the captors locked and loaded. I was waiting and prepared for the SEALs. Something told me that surely the US Government would do something. If not before our release, then after our departure. There were hundreds of cuts to hide a SEALs raft loaded with a team to capture these pirates after they dropped us off. But no, the US Government didn't do anything to try and catch these criminals. It was shocking. I had been expecting the US Navy SEALs every day.

When they felt it was safe, they would take the round out of the chamber and put their rifles back on safe, and then we would speed back up, and our nerves would calm back down. I looked at HiLo and told him to look back at Seamar. This crazy man tied the handles of the 75HP Yamahas together. He was standing between them, steering with his legs, and had his arms in the air like he was surfing.

Crazy, scary shit as anything could have happened. The rivers are so polluted, loaded with logs, oil pollutants, waste, trash, you name it, and it was floating around. If we had crashed, I would have drowned or died in the hospital from infections from the river.

Just like I have told everyone that has asked and some that didn't want to listen, these guys are like Olympic athletes. It was sad that so much athletic talent was wasted. Well, we finally arrived on the edge of the drop-off point, which was on the edge of a village along the river. Again, Seaman got on the phone with the negotiators and told them where to meet us. And again, we waited; the rescuers said they were about 15 minutes out, which turned into 45 minutes.

We sat with the bow pushed on the bank of the river. Apparently, we arrived at mosquito feeding time. I would say the mosquitoes drank about ½ a pint of blood out of me, and I would say the rest of the men were drained with about the same amount, give or take. Do you want to talk about no discipline? All of us in both boats were scratching, slapping, and bitching. A few pirates were happy to be back in cell reception and were busy making and receiving phone calls to their many girlfriends.

Finally, we saw a series of flashing lights, the agreed-upon signal, and we sailed forward about 1,500 feet up the river to what looked like an old warehouse. It was so dilapidated, there were holes in the walls, places where you could see boards missing, and the doors were open. Not a place we wanted to go inside.

Seamar and our rescuers were on the phone arguing about where we should dock the boat. Then, finally, Seamar ordered the boat to the bank, and the driver just slammed the bow, where I was sitting on the rope and with metal jammed up next to me, into the jagged metal dock with a huge thump.

Three pirates got out of the boat and made their way up and over the river bank to make the money exchange. From where the speedboat was, we couldn't see what was happening, but we heard a lot of screaming and hollering. Next, we saw Seaman and one of the others coming back with backpacks. Seaman sat the packs down and pulled out the ransom money. Then, with flashlights on, Seaman counted the money while we sat there anxiously waiting. I think we were all counting along with him. All of us in the boat were anxious. The captors wanted to go home, we wanted to go home, and he's just counting money. And it was short. It was like 2 million Naira ($4,625.67 US dollars) short of the agreed amount.

We were as mad about this as the pirates. It was terrible because the mood in the boat changed instantly. It went from being happy that it was almost over; and reverted to craziness. HiLo and I were back to wondering if we were about to die because someone either stole some of the money or couldn't count when they sent the money.

The two went back up and over the river bank to talk to

Seamar and the rescuers. All we could hear back at the boat were some Nigerians screaming and begging not to get hit. We were all sitting nervously. While waiting, one of the other pirates decided it was time to search HiLo and me again and took everything away except our medications. I tried to keep my handwritten notes on the cardboard I had found, but he found them and took them from me.

Finally, after about five more minutes, Seamar came down and started screaming at us to get out of the boat. He was mad, which is never good. He ordered us to walk partway up the riverbank. Then he ordered us to get down on the ground. He chambered a round in his weapon and yelled for us to lie face down in the dirt. With him being so angry, I knew it wasn't a good time to get in one last "screw-you." So we did as we were ordered and laid down, face down, on the bank of the river. Seaman and the other guy came down past us, and then Seamar joined them in the boat.

One of the most beautiful sounds I have ever heard was when we heard that boat engine rev up and take off in the opposite direction. We looked and thanked God they were gone and out of our lives.

It was not over, though.

## CHAPTER THIRTEEN

# Taken to Freedom

The three guys who came to do the exchange were waiting for us as we ran up the river bank. Once we were up and over, the rescuers ran to meet us. They rushed us along the edges of the warehouses and down dark, quiet paths. Finally, we crossed in front of a dimly lit church and over to a circle drive. There we were placed in an SUV. The rescuers wasted no time, and we headed out of there.

We met up with another car that was with the rescuers. It was bizarre; one of the men had called his chief and was crying. "Sir, they beat us badly and stole three Blackberrys and an iPad."

I looked at HiLo, and HiLo looked back at me. Instinctively, we both knew what the other was thinking. We communicated with an eye roll and shoulder shrug. We did not even need to say a word. But had we, it would have been, "Who would bring three Blackberrys and an iPad on a ransom exchange? Guess what, stupid. You are meeting up with a bunch of criminals who kidnapped two Americans, shot and destroyed a US-flagged vessel, and hijacked and stole from three shrimp boats. You think you probably should have left them at home?"

We just shook our heads and moved on. Next, we transferred to another car and discovered that the driver of the new vehicle was the Nigerian man we had talked to on the phone earlier.

He introduced himself to us, and we learned he was a Nigerian chief. At this point, I stopped hating all Nigerians and felt the feelings I had before this. So we are riding back to a hotel with chief Austin (a local tribal chief in Nigeria).

Once we settled in the new vehicle and were putting space between the river and us, I asked HiLo, "I wonder if our Nigerian manager sent any cigarettes or money for us, or at least a strong drink."

It had been dark out by the time we transferred into the car, and I didn't check who was in the vehicle for some reason. So after saying that, imagine my surprise when our Nigerian manager says, "I'm here," on the other side of HiLo.

I immediately apologized and asked for his forgiveness explaining I was under tremendous stress. He laughed it off and said no worries.

Once we arrived at the hotel, they escorted us straight to the chief's room. The room was very basic, as you would expect in this area of the world. We were still in Bayelsa State. However, the chief did have a bigger room. There were places to sit and a table to sit at to eat. It was an incredible culture shock after the past eighteen days. The chief welcomed us again, our Nigerian manager was there, and the three men from the rescue joined us. They explained that it was unsafe for us to travel in this region at night, and we would stay in the hotel overnight.

Our manager asked if we were hungry, and we said absolutely yes. Then, he asked us if we wanted a drink, and I said yes, Jack and Coke. HiLo wanted a Heineken. About fifteen minutes later, after small talk, someone walks in with plenty of beer, a whole bottle of Jack for me, and some cigarettes.

After a drink or two, they finally got me on the phone with my manager in the US. I could not talk. I was so excited and overwhelmed to hear another American voice. I started crying for the first time since that fateful morning of October 23. I couldn't talk. I just couldn't. Every time I tried to say a word, it came out in cries.

The US manager decided to give us a few minutes to acclimate and then called back. While speaking to our US manager, he said he had notified our wives and families that we were safe. They were waiting for us to call when we could. I cried again but finally got out a thank you and asked him to ask my wife to wait one more day to talk to me. I knew it would be impossible to talk to anyone I loved if I couldn't speak to him.

He told me it would not be a problem and told me, "Captain, we will talk later. You would be surprised to find out how many people were involved."

We went back to drinking and smoking and thanking and talking. We told what we could to the chief and swapped stories. Chief Austin asked us for some of the captors' names; one of the names stuck out, and that was Blackie. He said he was amazed at hearing that name because Blackie was the name of their leader that the Nigerian Government had just killed. We told him we didn't know which one was Blackie, but we were told their leader was killed.

He asked us if we had received the food they sent us, and we told him no, we didn't get it. But our captors certainly did. He said I think it was Seamar that met with him and Seamar explained to the chief that he wasn't involved in it but that he knew who was, and he knew where we were and would make sure that we got the food.

After a few drinks, smokes, and some food, we all talked in Chief Austin's room, sharing how things were for both sides. I asked chief Austin about the Nigerian Government. I was surprised not to see either Nigerian or US forces today. If the Nigerian or the US Government wanted to stop the hijackings and catch the militants, why didn't they have the Navy waiting hidden in an ambush and arrest the pirates after our release?

With all the creeks twisting and turning like spaghetti noodles, it would seem that someone, out of all the people watching us, would have done something. It would have been so easy. Or even drop a missile on our last known camp sometime during the night after we were gone. It was dark out and would have been easy to spot.

The lack of action leads me to believe that the Nigerian Government was complicit with the piracy, as our training had indicated. They do not care if the piracy stops. If the Nigerian Government wanted it to stop, they would address the piracy.

When the Somalian piracy was out of control, we saw the creation of Combined Task-Force-151 (CTF 151), also known as Combined Maritime Forces (CMF 151), to work in conjunction with NATO's Operation Ocean Shield. CTF 151 was a coalition of 20 countries contributing to the force, including the U.S., Canada, Denmark, France, Japan, The Republic of Korea, The Netherlands, Pakistan, Singapore, Thailand, and the United Kingdom, established in 2009. CTF 151 is to counter piracy and protect maritime commerce in areas including the Arabian Sea, Gulf of Oman, Gulf of Aden, Somali Basin, and the southern Red Sea in response to at least 219 attacks that occurred in the region in 2010, with 49 successful hijackings, according to the International Maritime Bureau (IMB)[3]. Somali pirates ships in the Gulf of Aden, along Somalia's eastern coastline, and outward into the Indian Ocean.

One of those kidnappings included the US-flagged ship *Maersk Alabama* on April 9, 2009. The vessel was under the authority of Captain Richard Phillips. It was the first US-flagged ship to be hijacked since 1822. Four pirates boarded the ship. During an altercation, one of the pirates was injured and taken hostage. The pirates had the Captain, and the crew tried to arrange to give back the hostage and a lifeboat in exchange for the Captain.

The pirates agreed, and their friend was released, but they forced Captain Phillips to go with them at the last minute. The

---

3   https://combinedmaritimeforces.com/ctf-151-counter-piracy/

pirates used the radio system on board the lifeboat to contact four other foreign vessels that fellow pirates had hijacked. The four ships converged on their fellow pirates in the lifeboat. On those other ships were fifty-four additional hostages from China, Germany, Russia, the Philippines, Tuvalu, Indonesia, and Taiwan.

The US Navy destroyer *USS Bainbridge* and the frigate *USS Halyburton* responded to the hostage situation. During the negotiations, the American ships agreed to take Abduwali Muse on board to meet with elders from his clan to negotiate the release of Phillips.

On April 12, 2009, The US Navy Seals, snipers of Red Squadron, part of the Naval Special Warfare Development Group, engaged and killed the remaining three pirates in the lifeboat and recovered Captain Phillips. Muse was arrested. Muse is believed to be the first person to be charged with piracy in American courts since 1885. Muse was sentenced to thirty-three years and nine months in US federal prison.[4]

Counter-piracy patrols near Somalia are to complement mariners' self-protection measures. Increased patrols and proactive efforts by ships have reduced attacks in the Gulf of Aden. That is all on the opposite side of Africa. There were no such efforts (at that time) on the Nigerian side of Africa in the Gulf of Guinea. I heard ships sailing through Somalia use load speakers and blaring Britney Spears's music to fight off pirates. The Somalis hated Americans so much that it drove them crazy, which would not work on Nigerian pirates because they love the American culture.

We discussed how pirates had hijacked the *C-Endeavour*, and now pirates had hijacked the *C-Retriever*. At what point will there be a Combined Maritime Forces on the Nigerian side of Africa?

Another thing that struck me funny was Chief Austin told us that he had happened to meet the leader Seamar. I am guessing

4  https://www.reuters.com/article/us-usa-somalia-pirate/somali-pirate-handed-33-year-sentence-by-u-s-court-idUSTRE71F60H20110216

this was during one of Seamar's trips to the village. Seamar had told him that he wasn't involved in the kidnapping but knew where we were. So Seamar told Chief Austin that if he would give him some Naira, he would, out of kindness, buy some food and supplies and bring them out to the swamp for us.

It was getting late, and Chief Austin didn't want to let us go but reluctantly did. Before he did, he asked us if we wanted separate rooms. My answer to him was no way! I slept with my little buddy for eighteen days, and he was not leaving my side until we returned to the states.

So we got up and carried our food trays, beer, and Jack to our room. I don't know what I did next; being a biker, I probably gave HiLo a big hug and kiss. We ate a small amount of some delicious chicken, trying not to overeat and make ourselves sick. Then we each took a turn in the shower. In actual water, not that nasty creek water, not the small amount of rainwater we had collected to bathe. The shower had clean water and good water pressure, there was soap, and it felt amazing to be clean.

After a while, as we did every night in the swamps, HiLo said, "Good night, Mr. Stone."

I told him, "Good night, Mr. HiLo."

Laying down in the hotel bed was a treat. It was nice to be in a bed. Not on moldy foam. It also felt great to stretch out, both with our own space. We both passed out quickly.

## Captain Wren Thomas' Wife, Rhonda Thomas

## November 9, 2013

*Another Saturday morning, frustration was setting in. We know nothing happens over the weekend, so we probably would not hear anything all weekend.*

*The FBI ladies called me at about 2:00 p.m. and said they were* coming to the house. I panicked. They would have told me on the phone if it were rescue news. I just knew this was going to be bad news. I had to get rid of Ruby and her friend fast. I couldn't let them bring me bad news with Ruby in the house. So I called the Robinsons, and Lisa came to pick up the girls and take them shopping and to a movie.

The FBI ladies showed up at 3:00 p.m. and asked for a conference call. I had to text everyone and tell them we were going online for the call. Sheri, Judy, and Uncle Denny got on the call, and I think Kari too. I was about to faint because I felt this would be bad news. I texted Brenda while we were on the call and asked her to come over. Right NOW. I couldn't hear her on the call. Uncle Denny must have noticed the strain in my voice because he showed up before the call was over.

The call began, and Kathy explained that negotiations were back on track. The kidnappers were again talking to the negotiating team. They felt as though this would end very soon. While everyone was talking on the conference call, Kathy got a text, and I read her face, she showed the text to Sue, and I held out my hand to take her phone. I knew before she said the words that Tommy and HiLo were safe!!

Tommy and HiLo have been rescued after a ransom payment. However, at the place where Tommy and HiLo were, it was not safe to travel until the sun was up. Therefore, they could not be transported safely to Prodeco Camp until the following day.

The FBI didn't tell anyone on the conference call about the rescue. Instead, they wanted to tell Judy in person.

I called Blake first, as I had promised him. Then, I called Brenda, and she wouldn't answer; I called Sheri and asked Uncle Denny to call my parents and sisters.

Aunt Kay showed up and cried hard. I kept trying to call Brenda, and she didn't answer, so I got in the car and drove to her house. I ran and busted through the door to tell her. Her phone was dead, *and she was painting her living room. Her friend was there, and it was an explosion of emotion.*

*I left there and went home. The phones went nuts. Adrienne gave me flight information to get there, and Joe called me to share the joy. He said that Wren had talked to Brent and that Wren told him to let me know that he would call me in the morning when he could speak and that he loved me very much. I still was a little apprehensive and didn't trust them, and I wasn't sure my husband had left that message for me but later learned that this was precisely what Tommy had told Brent to tell me.*

*I could bring Ruby, but I decided it wasn't a good idea. I had no idea where I was going or how long I would be gone. I did not know when Tommy would arrive, where I would stay, none of that. I still didn't know if he was injured or what condition he would be in. The FBI had coached me about his homecoming. All of their information was the opposite of what I should have done.*

*The rest of the night was chaos, finding someone to care for the animals, packing, and preparing for the trip. Uncle Denny came to take care of the animals, and Ruby went to Missy's house. I had to be in Bloomington early the following day for a flight to New Orleans. I left the truck at the airport because I wasn't sure where and when I would return with Tommy. So many things were unsure at this time. I talked to Blake and Dillon, who planned to meet us Monday morning at the office, but I still didn't know where, when, or what time. I stayed up all night, dusted and vacuumed the house, finished packing my things, and stared at the moon.*

## Captain Wren Thomas' Son, Dillon Thomas

## Day 18

*I went home after work; my brother Blake texted me on the way. Being a nervous wreck at work, I could only imagine the worst. Is my Dad dead? Could they not come to terms over the ransom? The worst of things were flying around in my head. Finally, I arrived home. Blake ran to me, hugged me, and said they got him, and he is alive.*

*These are the best two words I've heard in my life! Then, finally, one of my best friends was back; I couldn't wait to hear his voice and see him.*

*After a big night of talking to friends and family, I just wanted to hear his voice. So the first thing the following day, Dad called me, and tears just rolled down my face like Niagara Falls. That was the happiest moment of my life. He told me he loved me, was sorry, and that I could come to see him the following day.*

*The stress, headaches, and sleepless nights were over. My Dad is safe and is coming back home where he needs to be.*

## Captain Wren Thomas

## November 10, 2013

Even though I thought last night would be the best sleep ever, I passed out for about three hours and then woke up and stared at the walls. I sat up and smoked half a pack of cigarettes, lost in my thoughts. Then my Nigerian manager knocked on the door, startling me. He told me we would leave for Port Harcourt in about fifteen minutes. I woke HiLo. We got dressed and headed to the parking lot to get into the SUVs. Ready to head out for the next leg of our long journey home.

Chief Austin and my Nigerian manager were mad because the rest of the rescue team still weren't awake. It became the norm, with the bosses screaming at the group once they arrived. We loaded up and headed to the office in Port Harcourt, arriving about two hours later. It felt wonderful to be back inside the gates, our home turf, and a place where we felt relatively safe.

## Port Harcourt

The first person who met us when we returned to our office was our company security officer. I gave him a very long and huge hug. As he was also a biker and an excellent friend, I didn't want to let him go. He welcomed us back and asked if I wanted a cup of coffee. I told him please that I would love coffee as long as it was community. He said it was, and then he handed me my coffee cup.

What he gave me was no ordinary cup. This cup had my stepdaughter Ruby's picture on it. It was a cup she gave me the Christmas before. I lost it and again could not stop crying. He told me when he went to the vessel to collect our belongings, that cup was the only thing he didn't pack. He told everyone that he was going to hand it to me personally. I was overwhelmed by what he had done, staying certain I would be back.

He walked us inside, and we sat down to an incredible breakfast our American manager in Nigeria had prepared. It was wonderful. He told me that he and everyone that knew me were freaking out for the first five days. They had not heard from us and didn't know how I would react.

Some of our friends thought the biker and Marine would have come out in me and that I probably killed some of the captors. Others thought maybe I had done the smart thing and stayed calm. (Come to find out, everyone who knows me was thinking the same thing that with Wren, things can go two different ways). It was an excellent welcome.

Our company security officer and American manager ensured we had clean clothes. Our manager had ironed the clothes himself. They also had any toiletries we would need. The crying continued. I was happy. HiLo and I talked when still in the swamp and decided we would tell everyone to leave us alone until we landed in the states.

Well, that went away with the Tribal chief that came to get us.

While at the office, we were allowed to shower again and change into our new clothes. Next, we went to the SOS Clinic, where we had physicals and blood tests for malaria. All of the tests came out good except my jungle rot. Finally, I had an antibiotic ointment to treat the infection.

Both of us wanted to go down to the vessel and see it and the crew and tell everyone bye. But instead, we were rushed to Port Harcourt Airport to travel to Lagos.

Time started going slow at this point. The wait at Port Harcourt Airport seemed like days instead of a few hours, and the flight to Lagos seemed hours long when it was only forty-five minutes.

## Lagos & the FBI

We arrived in Lagos, where the FBI met us. The FBI said that they had managed to keep the press away. So we went through the introductions and the welcomes and headed to the US Embassy. When we arrived at the embassy, there were more introductions and welcomes. They asked us if HiLo and I could be separated for debriefings. We both agreed that it would be ok. They treated us well and said if we needed anything, ask. They also said we could have dinner and drinks at their club after the interview. So I went my way, HiLo went his, and we did our interviews.

We went to a hotel-type room, and again they apologized for having to do this debriefing. The Agent said conducting the debriefing as soon as possible after our release was essential.

I told them, "Please, no apologies. It's necessary."

Plus, I needed to talk. I talked, and the Agents took notes. I told them everything I could remember. While talking, I noticed that I would get lost. I got lost a lot. I knew I had attention deficit disorder (ADD), but this was worse. It was like talking and just stopping because I would forget where I was going with what I was trying to say. That scared me, as I knew my head was messed up. They told me not to worry about it, as they understood. I gave them so much information, and after about an hour, they took a break, and I drank some coffee.

They had left the room, and when they returned, they asked me if I would like to end the interview and get some dinner. The Agents also said HiLo had completed his debriefing.

I told them no, I didn't want to end it yet, that they wanted to talk, so we were going to talk. After about another thirty to forty-five minutes, I was through. I told them everything I knew, names, faces, body types, ages, tattoos, Storytime's prosthetic, Storytime's seemingly military background, and everything we had learned from Dee. We knew they enslaved people or prospects (community boys).

As the debriefing progressed, I drew pictures of the two camps where we had been held and told them about my Skoal can trail. I shared with them information on the habits of our captors. I explained how the pirates acted and what they wore (basically, they ran around all day in my underwear that they had stolen from the ship). I told them our captors had made many trips to the local village. We talked about all the marijuana and crack cocaine they would smoke. I tried to give them as much as I could.

I told them that our kidnapping appeared to be part of a much larger, more significant organization than what the captors led us to believe. I explained that one day, without our captors knowing, HiLo and I watched a video that they were watching on a cell phone. From what we could see, hundreds of men were celebrating and chanting. The same chants that we had heard Preacher chant 100 times before.

I was finally done and was ready for a drink, so we went down to the Embassy Club, and I ordered a Coke. I guessed I could handle another Jack and Coke but decided it best not to since I had drunk three-quarters of a bottle the night before. So I drank my coke, and HiLo drank his Heineken. We did this for about an hour until it was time to go to the Lagos airport.

We loaded up the vans and went to the airport. As soon as we arrived, they whisked us away to a VIP lounge where we smoked and drank some more. HiLo was getting pretty drunk by this time and was having an in-depth conversation with one of the FBI Agents. I was cracking up about what they were talking about and couldn't believe it. They were talking about their high school years.

## Finally able to call his wife

We left this lounge and moved to another more private lounge. It was here we finally called home. I was excited I finally got to talk to my wife. As soon as she answered the phone I said "supppppppp," and she knew it was I. I don't remember the conversation, but it was great. I was so happy to hear her voice.

It had been nineteen days since I had talked to her. We usually at least get a text from each other every day. I missed her and was ready to get home and hold her. I missed my kids, my Mom, my Grandmother, my Sisters, friends and family, my club brothers, my dogs, my horses, my bed, and my house (that we had just built a year before). I was ready to get home. And I knew I would grab a saddle and jump up on my horse Samson as soon as I got home. I needed to ride, and it was too cold to ride the Harley.

## Captain Wren Thomas' Wife, Rhonda Thomas

## November 10, 2013

*I left Bloomington airport and headed for New Orleans early that morning. Just the second I was boarding the airplane, my phone rang, and it was Tommy!*

*I answered, and he said, "suppppppp." It was the happiest moment ever. He told me briefly that he was ok and he was at the airport getting ready to come home. I wanted to talk to him forever, but the flight crew dragged me onto the airplane and said that if I didn't board, I had to get another flight.*

*We cried together for a moment and then said goodbye until tomorrow morning. I landed in Atlanta, GA, and called Blake and Dillon again. It was a long layover, and I was anxious to get there, get to bed and get to my husband. I had met Karen and Adrienne a few times, and I knew to look for them at the airport, but when I landed in New Orleans and got off the plane, all the ladies looked alike. I couldn't find either of them and started to panic. Finally, Karen called and told me to meet her at baggage claim, Adrienne picked us up at the curb, and we headed toward Galliano.*

*I thought we were going to the hotel, but Adrienne took us to her house, and we all had a meal together. I got to meet HiLo's wife for the first time. Joe and Richard were there, along with Adrienne, Karen, and their husbands. I was so tired from a long trip, and the last thing I felt like doing was socializing with these people.*

*It was a celebration dinner to them, but to HiLo's wife and I, we weren't ready to celebrate until we had our husbands home. HiLo's wife and I were the only smokers, so while those people were inside talking, we were outside smoking and talking about our men coming home.*

*Adrienne took me to the hotel at about 10:00 p.m. That night I just looked out the window and waited for the call. Joe said they weren't sure when the flight would arrive, but he would call and wake us and take us to the hangar to meet them.*

*I wanted so badly for Blake and Dillon to come there, but nobody would tell me where to have them meet us. The Chouest people kept telling me it was a private landing strip about five minutes up the road. I felt that the flight would come at 6:00 a.m. since the flight from Nigeria to Atlanta always arrives around 5:00 a.m.*

*I knew the FBI had promised a quick trip through customs and directly to the Chouest private plane. I figured the flight from Atlanta to Galliano was only an hour, so I just prepared myself to be ready by then.*

## CHAPTER FOURTEEN

# Return to America

### Captain Wren Thomas

### Flight to America

Finally, they notified us that it was time to go to our gate, as we were boarding before priority boarding. We walked to the gate, and until now, everything went smoother than ever as the FBI made sure we rushed through everything. However, arriving at our gate, a Nigerian woman would not let us through. She started fussing about how no one notified her about anything, and until she was, we weren't going anywhere.

After a few phone calls and a manager arriving, we were allowed to board. We were flying back accompanied by our company security officer. We got on the plane, and we were seated in first class. Once we learned that, HiLo and I started laughing out loud. The whole time we were hostages, we joked that we would sit in coach on the way home. Unfortunately, something happened with the tickets and our Security Officer had to sit in coach. That sucked as we thought he would be sitting with us where we could talk.

As it turned out, it was okay because HiLo and I ate and slept the entire flight to Atlanta. I had dinner on the plane, stretched out in my chair, and passed out. The chair was perfect, and I had plenty of room, even as tall as I am—finally, a nice bed and good-smelling blankets. The only thing I could think of the entire way to Atlanta was how it would play out. We made it through eighteen days of being held by militants, and now we will crash in the middle of the Atlantic. Talking to HiLo later, he said he was thinking the same thing.

## Veterans Day

## November 11, 2013

Our flight landed in Atlanta around 05:30 a.m. Finally, we were on American soil. Before I disembarked the plane, I cornered one of the stewards and said to him, "Sir, I am not sure if you know who I am, but if you would please pass on to the pilots a big thank you for getting us back home safely. Also, please thank the entire crew for their kindness."

It was tough to get out all of these words. After a big hug, we said our goodbyes. Delta Airlines at its best. We didn't realize it was Veterans Day until someone told us, "Happy Veterans Day." What a day to land in the U.S. HiLo is a Navy Vet, and I am a Marine Corps Vet.

Our stay didn't last long in Atlanta because the FBI whisked us through customs and immigration. Then we were taken to a van and transported to a private terminal to board the company jet. So HiLo, our company security officer, and I were finally on the last leg of our voyage.

During that flight, I watched the screen with a map of where the jet was and the flight data. Once again, we were waiting for the other shoe to drop. We were sure that the plane would crash on our way to Louisiana. We finally landed in Galliano, Louisiana, and taxied to the hangar. We looked out the port holes to see our wives and managers, and everyone had a big smile waiting in anticipation for us to disembark the plane.

## Captain Wren Thomas' Wife, Rhonda Thomas

### November 11, 2013

*Joe called me at about 5:00 a.m., and I was already showered, dressed, and waiting for all of them. HiLo's wife came down next, and we all boarded a Mercedes limo van driven by Ben to the airstrip. We got there minutes before the plane landed.*

*My heart was pounding as it landed, and we watched our men get off the airplane. Then, finally, Tommy got off, and I ran to him and hugged him. I wanted to cry but didn't want to cry in front of these people. So I decided to cry later. He was so thin, and although happy to be home, I couldn't help but feel horrible for him, knowing that he lost that weight by being nearly starved by the kidnappers.*

## Captain Wren Thomas

Finally! HiLo and I walked down the ladder from the airplane, and my wife ran and jumped into my arms. We hugged for what seemed like an eternity. It was nice to be home. I hugged everyone I could, as I was overwhelmed with happiness.

HiLo introduces me to his wife, saying, "Honey, this is Captain Wren. He is the man I have been sleeping with the last eighteen days."

We all got a laugh out of that one.

It was nice to hug the managers even though there were points during the last eighteen days when all I wanted to do was beat the living tar out of them. They did well. But, when you are in the swamp, the only one you are talking to is a Nigerian manager; you wonder, does anyone even care that we are out here?

We didn't know that we had our office was working around the clock and losing many hours of sleep. Professional negotiators were doing what they do. The FBI was doing what they do.

It did seem odd to us that the press wasn't there to cover our return. We didn't understand why. We were told it was in our 'best interest' not to talk to the press. We believed them, as these were people we trusted. (Later, I figured out that talking to the media would have been best for us, and the reason we couldn't speak to the press was not our best interest but the company's.)

It is one of the first of many times the company thought about their best interest and didn't give a shit about our best interest. Well, for now, it was what it was.

We jumped into a very nice custom van provided by the company and headed to our hotel room for a nice shower and clean clothes. My wife brought me all brand new clothes, knowing I would need them.

About thirty minutes later, we were on our way to the office. Arriving at the office, we got more welcome homes and some very welcoming hugs. Then, we went up to the cafeteria and had breakfast and coffee. It was one of the best breakfasts I have ever had. Our company chef went all out. It was wonderful, and I didn't mind being a pig. Unfortunately, I didn't eat as much as I wanted as my stomach still had gotten back to normal from the lack of nutrition.

We went downstairs and had a few more smokes before the next interview with Dionne and Dino Chouest. I was told during my debriefing that I would be able to talk to the other crews and that I would be able to join in the process of making changes to policies and making the vessels more secure.

After speaking with them, we were going to be debriefed by managers. It was too much. We had been through so much at that point. I figured we had only slept twelve broken hours in the past ninety-six hours. So now we will be debriefed by our company.

The debriefings were going to be done by two managers, our company security officer, our company designated person ashore, and one of the men from the negotiating team. HiLo having to drive back home, went first. I knew he had a long journey, so I figured it best. While he was in there, his wife told us that she planned to have his club brothers meet them about an hour from home, bringing his bike so he could ride into town in his style. I thought that was the greatest thing in the world.

We sat outside and waited and smoked. We talked to the two incredible women who helped our wives get through it. I have to say they went well beyond their regular jobs. I will never forget all they did for my wife and little girl. Like I told them and still feel today, thank you is not good enough to describe how good it felt to know they were there for my family. Finally, after a couple of hours, it was my turn to be debriefed.

I hugged HiLo and told him goodbye. It was odd to be apart. However, the bond of surviving what we did together was powerful.

I was taken into a conference room and sat at a conference table with the rest of the men doing the debriefing. The very first thing I was asked was did I mind if they recorded the session. I told them no, I didn't care.

We spent about an hour going over the same shit I just went over with the FBI the day before. I was fine until It came to the point that I was questioned about two plots I had made on my chart and the time they were made. I had made a mistake on the time or the plot, or I took the latitude and longitude from a different GPS that may have had errors.

I had two GPS units to choose from and typically used both. This was when I got upset. I was drilled on when I went to bed, and I told them between 11:30 p.m. and 11:45 p.m. I felt they were accusing me of lying because they kept on me why my handwriting continued into the next day at 12:01 a.m. I explained that out of respect, I usually would start my chief officer's log for him if I knew what we were doing at the end of my watch would be the same as his start. This way, he only has to fill in the Latitude and Longitude at his 12:01 a.m. position.

Well, this wasn't good enough, and it seemed that this was turning into an interrogation instead of a debriefing. I was getting angry, and my temper was flaring.

They finally decided it was time to take a break. So all but one of my managers left the room. I walked up to the manager and told him that if they accused me of wrongdoing, to let me know now. If they intended to interrogate me, this interview was now over, and they would be hearing from my attorney.

He assured me that this wasn't the case. Come to find out that between the time we were taken and the time the boat got back to the dock three and a half days later, the crew managed to sell 100 tons of fuel. The client (Chevron), along with the office, wanted answers.

That response didn't make me happy. I didn't like being interrogated. After a few hours of this, they finally concluded the interrogation. They asked me to make a list of what property I was missing.

I told them I had made enough money to replace everything I had lost. Come to find out, when I received most of my belongings from Nigeria, the genius pirates that kidnapped us didn't take my diamond wedding band, two other silver rings, or my USMC ring. That's funny; they stole my under drawers but left my jewelry. The crew probably took anything else that was missing after we were kidnapped.

After the interrogation/debriefing, my wife and I were provided a company car, and we headed for Lafayette to see my two sons and grandsons. On the trip to Lafayette, my wife and I took the time to talk. We talked and talked and talked.

I told her my story, and she told me hers. We don't usually talk a lot, not because of problems; we don't talk like many couples do.

It's just the way we both are. But, we talked this day and talked all the way to Lafayette. She explained that friends and family, my club brothers, the FBI, the hostage negotiating team men, and the two wonderful ladies from my office loaded our house.

Everyone was great. It was overwhelming, but my wife appreciated everything. My eldest sister Brenda packed a few bags and camped at my house for a few weeks. She provided a lot of help around the house, did a lot of research, and helped keep track of everything going on.

## Captain Wren Thomas' Wife, Rhonda Thomas

## November 11, 2013

*The van picked us up about forty-five minutes later to take us to the Chouest offices. Blake and Dillon were on the way from Lafayette, and when they called for Tommy, he told Blake to turn around and go home. Tommy told him we would come to Lafayette tonight when he finished.*

*While they debriefed Tommy, Adrienne took me to get one of their company cars and gave me our hotel reservation for Lafayette. Tommy and I left there and drove to Lafayette. Again we talked the entire way there.*

*My husband told me about his experience. So much of it was what I expected. Some of it was shocking. I was so grateful that he had prepared me for what was possible before this happened. I was just so thankful that he was alive.*

*I was amazed at how much he talked and wanted to say. The FBI team had coached me much about what to expect, and they were very wrong. They said he would be detached, not want to share all this, and told us to understand that he would want to be alone, not have a crowd around. They warned us that he would not want to deal with the media.*

*My husband wanted his family and friends around, his deserved homecoming, and a parade. He wanted to share all the details with everyone.*

*I have told Brenda many times I take full responsibility for this part. I should not have listened to anyone, and I should have just gone with my gut instinct. I feel horrible that he didn't get all the attention he deserves.*

*When we got to Lafayette, we checked into our hotel and went to Blake's house. It was terrific for Tommy to spend with his boys, even though very short. They visited, and we all went out for pizza.*

*We returned to the hotel, and Dillon and Caitlyn spent the night there. Then, finally, we all went to bed. Tommy needed to rest. He was obviously exhausted, and I was worried about him. He looked pale and weak. He wrapped his arms around me that night, and I finally wept.*

## Captain Wren Thomas

We arrived in Lafayette at my oldest son Blake's house with Dillon, my younger son, on his way. It was an excellent reception with lots of hugs and a few tears. Blake, my daughter-in-law Amanda, my two grandsons Blaze and Hunter (now I have three grandsons with the addition of Lucas), and Blake's mother-in-law Zelda, met me.

When Dillon arrived, he grabbed me and cried, and I cried. It was hard. Dillon is just like me. Blake has a heart of gold, and it doesn't take much to bring us to tears. Dillon is the biggest at 6 ft. 7 inches and 280 pounds, I'm 6 ft. 2 inches and 265 pounds, and Blake at 6 ft. and around 200 pounds. All of us are just big teddy bears.

We spent a little time talking, and I asked everyone to excuse the boys and myself to go outside and talk. I told them some of what happened and how it happened. Then I asked them how they were doing and how things went for them while I was captive

They said during the time I was a hostage; they kept calling the office to get more information. The office refused to take their calls. Finally, the office told my sons they wouldn't talk to them as they couldn't prove they were talking to my sons. My sons are on my Life Insurance Policies with their social security numbers, and Dillon is still on my medical insurance. The FBI knew they were my sons. Every news media in the USA knew they were my sons. But ECO wouldn't talk to them, as they didn't believe they were my sons.

The press had contacted Dillon, the boy's mom, my ex-wife Jenny, and Jenny's Mom, to get more information. The FBI also convinced them not to talk to the press. I felt terrible that ECO wouldn't provide any information to my sons while I was being held hostage.

It is the same thing Rhonda and my Illinois family went through. News crews surrounded the end of my driveway. The family was convinced not to talk to the press.

After having pizza with the family, Rhonda, Dillon, and I headed for our hotel suite that the company graciously provided. I finally got to meet Dillon's current girlfriend. She is a wonderful young lady.

We finally fell asleep in another beautiful bed. We woke the following day, Monday, November 12th, and passed out hugs and tears. Then we went to Blake's house to pass out more hugs. My poor Blaze cried his heart out, not wanting us to leave.

Rhonda and I loaded up the rental car and headed back to Galliano. I found time to call my club Brother Troy (Rugrat) to thank him for all the club had done to help and to let him know I was okay and would be home soon.

## Captain Wren Thomas' Son, Dillon Thomas

*My Stepmom and Dad came to Lafayette to come and see us. I had never smiled so BIG in all my life. No Superman, no Batman, but he is my Hero, and I will love him until I die. The sacrifice he took of going offshore for half a year to another country and knowing the risks he is taking in these African waters only to provide for his family.*

*Thanks for all the sacrifices you make for your family Dad. It has always been appreciated and always will. We may live hundreds of miles away, but that doesn't make one difference. Just hearing your voice makes me feel like I am that much closer to you. I love you, Dad, and I hope the best for you out of this situation.*

## Captain Wren Thomas' Wife, Rhonda Thomas

## November 12, 2013

*We left the hotel early to go say goodbye to Blake, Blaze, and Hunter. But unfortunately, Amanda was already at work. So we drove back to Galliano, LA, and the office.*

*Tommy stopped and bought a huge bottle of Crown Royal for Tmel, Brent, Ben, and Warren. After that, he met with them again, and they wrapped it up. This time I didn't leave the room, although, from the look on Brent's face, he would have liked me to.*

*I didn't like what I was hearing from my husband about his interview the previous day, and I was recharged and ready if they intended to interrogate him any further. My husband is intelligent, strong, and handles himself well. I trusted that he could take this, but I was still worried that this guy sitting here wasn't all of my husband. I felt like his experience weakened him, and at that time, I knew now he was handling it well, but that day I just wasn't sure.*

*The job that I assigned myself was to protect him and get him home. So we left the office, and Ben took us to the airstrip to board the private jet for Champaign, IL. Kari and Randy went to Bloomington, got our truck, and parked at Willard airport for us. The club wanted to come to the airport, but we feared the media being there. Wow, again. I will go through the rest of my life regretting this.*

## Captain Wren Thomas

My Mom, Judy, and sisters Sheri, Brenda, and Kari were always helping. My cousin Kim had armbands that said "WCT3 Prayers going up, blessings coming down," and passed them out to everyone who wanted one. It made me so happy to know how far people went to help. Our neighbor tied a yellow ribbon around our mailbox. My office had their chef send food packages, and my good friend Meatball, a chef, and one of my club brothers sent over a tremendous amount of food.

My wife had plenty of help and plenty of love around her. My nephew Marshall and a friend of ours, Pat, came over to help clean horse stalls and help with chores. One of Rhonda's wonderful Uncles came over and helped as well. My nephew Cory borrowed us a critter cam so they could see and monitor the driveway.

What free time Rhonda did have, she spent putting together a book of my Great Grandmother and Grandfather and Grandmothers memoirs. My stepdaughter kept the FBI busy and the two men from the negotiating team by bringing them out to the barn and showing off her prized pony, Oscar, and making them watch her ride her 4-wheeler.

## CHAPTER FIFTEEN

# Home to Illinois

On the way back to the office from seeing my boys, I had second thoughts about how I had gone off in the office the day before during the debriefing. So I stopped at a store and grabbed the biggest and best bottle of Crown Royal I could find. Arriving at the office, I met with my managers, gave them the bottle, and apologized for how I talked to them. They were very understanding, and I think they appreciated the gift as they were all strung out from stress and lack of sleep. We talked awhile, and then Rhonda and myself were sent to the company jet to fly back home to Champaign, Illinois. The ride home was nice and smooth. We didn't talk a lot. I think we were both in shock from this finally being over.

Again, during the flight, I thought I was so close now that the plane would probably crash on the way to Champaign. This feeling sucked as it added a ton of stress. So during the flight, I grabbed a Coke and grabbed Rhonda a Diet Coke along with a snickers bar and just about everything else I could find to eat until we finally landed in Champaign.

When I talked with my club brother, he said the club wanted to meet us at the airport, but again we were convinced to keep everything quiet so the press wouldn't get alerted. So it was quiet, and it was cold. It wasn't cold for everyone, but it was freezing after being hot and sweaty in the humid swamp as long as I was. In the terminal, I was introduced to the FBI Agents who kindly helped my wife. We were given a room to talk in, and I gave them a summary of what happened and how it happened. After hugging and thanking each one of the agents, we headed home.

It was great to see my truck. My little sister Kari made sure it was professionally detailed and beautiful. It was wonderful. Finally, I was walking through the front door of my home, being attacked by my Lab Sasha and my Shitzu Lucy. They were all over me and excited as they missed their Daddy. I took a long shower and did some other things, and soon I had family coming over, and we talked.

Later, we visited my mother's house to visit my sisters, mother, and grandmother. We talked a little about what I went through and how it was for them. Then, Mom wanted to make plans for Thanksgiving because we had much to be thankful for.

## Captain Wren Thomas' Mother, Judy Davis-King

*On November 9, 2013, The FBI wanted us to all meet at our house. They had told us earlier things were moving along over there. When the FBI and his sisters arrived, they announced that both men had been released to their company. Oh, what a glorious day that was.*

*They said he would be flown to Louisiana for medical evaluations and debriefing with the FBI and his company. They flew his wife Rhonda down to meet him when he got off the plane. That was on November the 11. We all saw him on November 12 when they flew back to Illinois, his home state. Back to his family and country home that he so loved.*

## Captain Wren Thomas

## Home

The more I talked with the family, I developed a greater under-standing of how hard it was on them – not knowing and not being given many answers was really. Ruby watches "*Criminal Minds*" on TV and tells one of the agents that Penelope would have already had this all figured out.

On Tuesday, I decided it was time to get some fried chicken, so I visited my Aunt Linda, Uncle Terry, my cousin Kim, and her husband, Randy. I cried, and my Aunt and Cousin cried. I think I was about dehydrated from crying so much. We were at a bar in Roberts; it was all you can eat, and we ate.

I think it was Wednesday the next night. I finally got to go to my clubhouse and see my brothers. It was a welcome that I will never forget. Again, bikers like to hug, and some like to hug and give a kiss. Well, in my club there is a lot of this. I hugged each one of my brothers and sisters and club friends. I found out just how many prayers were going out to God for me.

I'm sure God was overwhelmed between my club, family, and the rest of the world. I cried when Troy told me again that he had never been to church and had never prayed but found it in his heart to pray for me. Meatball had the biggest ribeye steak cooked for me; it was delicious. It was cooked perfectly and wrapped with bacon – it was very tasty, as is everything he cooks.

I got very drunk that night between my Jim Beam and coke and all the toasts with shots of turkey, apple pie moonshine, and tequila. I hugged the toilet at home that night and had my two dogs protecting me.

One night, we had a great time in Peoria, IL; the Outlaws Motorcycle Club had a toy fundraiser with four or five bands and David Allen Coe. It was fun, and I needed it. I again got to see and hug many good friends and brothers. The Outlaws did a great thing that night, and I was happy to be a part of it. They are all very good men.

## Helping after tornadoes

A few days after I was home, the weather brought in high winds, rain, and tornadoes. A neighboring town, Gifford, was destroyed. I reached out to my brother-in-law and found out that friends and family of his needed help. I told him I had horses, 4-wheelers, a horse trailer, and a small trailer to haul things. I told him they were welcome to use any of it they needed. He thanked me but said they needed a helping hand in cleaning up.

I loaded up and headed out there, and there was overwhelming destruction. It was unbelievable. I helped with the cleanup and decided to run home and get my Polaris side by side to help with cleanup. I worked as long as my body let me that day and then went back the next. Picking up trash and sifting through debris looking for keepsakes was difficult. I couldn't help but think I didn't have it so bad after all.

A few days after the storms, our local bar, the Sidney Saloon, had a benefit concert with one of the popular local bands. A few of my club brothers showed up. The band decided to auction off a guitar, and Troy told me he said brother, whatever you bid, I will match it, so I'm like, cool. The bid got up to a couple of hundred dollars, and then I decided to make things happen and bid $400. Troy almost choked. I busted out laughing. It was fun, and it went to a good cause.

Being in a Motorcycle Club (MC) teaches you that when folks need help, you should be the first to give a hand. After what I had just been through, I needed to multiply the support given to my family and myself. Just like the Bible says, give, and you will receive tenfold. I did receive this, only backward. I was given tenfold and tried to give back more.

We spent days comparing stories, visiting people, answering phone calls, and eating. We did a lot of Christmas shopping.

After feeling the prayers and support from around the world during our captivity, I decided the best way to thank God was by getting involved in church again. I felt it was important to give back. So we looked for a new church home for the family, and after trying two different ones, we settled in at Stone Creek Church in Urbana, IL.

As Christmas was quickly approaching, I was able to provide presents to the needy. It was just one of the many things my church was doing at this time. It was significant to me as this was one thing I loved to do, help those in need.

I love Stone Creek but find it hard to sit through a sermon without having tears build in my eyes. I don't know if God has spoken to the Pastors and told them what to read, but every Sunday I have been, the sermon seems to be about me. Every word spoken hits me hard. I genuinely understand each sermon. It is very heartfelt.

## CHAPTER SIXTEEN

# First Anxiety Attack

### First anxiety attack

My family, Rhonda, and I talked and compared notes a lot. We are finding out just how many lies were told. It is unbelievable how it all went down. One of the biggest lies was that the vessel had so much damage that it had to be towed when the Nigerian crew finished both runs alone. It took three and a half days to get the ship back to Onne.

Here is a copy of an email from my manager for the West Africa Division of ECO.

*Good afternoon Wren.*

*Hope you had a good Thanksgiving and are enjoying some R&R.*

*Ben forwarded a copy of the mail you sent, and I would like to put your mind at ease. From all information we've gathered, this incident appears to be a random act of convenience. We don't believe the Retriever was specifically targeted, but rather a target of opportunity. You did nothing wrong!*

*The vessel arrived back in port with approximately 100,000 liters of fuel unaccounted for. Of course, all of the crew said they knew nothing about it. Upon arrival, fresh comet was on the decks near the sounding tubes. I doubt that would have still been there since the tanks were sounded before leaving port.*

*Since Ebenezer was in charge once you and HiLo were removed, I gave him the option to tell me what happened to the fuel and keep his job or the alternative. He said he didn't know. So I gave him a second chance, and he stuck to his story. Unfortunately, he chose the alternative. I hope you understand.*

*FYI we've received information from the SSS that they've arrested three militants. Supposedly they've confessed, even admitting how the ransom amount was split.*

*Ben said you didn't feel like speaking to anyone, but if and when you do, please call me or let me know a good time to call you. I would like to talk to you. I hope you will agree that I've always been straight with you, and I don't believe in BS. Take care!*

I found it interesting that they admitted how the ransom was split. To this day, I don't know where all the ransom money went. We don't know who was behind the kidnapping. It was an organized group with over one hundred men because we accidentally watched the pirates on facetime.

So who was responsible, and where did the money go to terrorism? Boko Haram is very active in the area. There were some reports that the Movement for the Emancipation of the Niger Delta (MEND) may have been partially responsible. Other reports indicated that the ransom funded Cameroon's African Marine Commando group.

These men were kidnapping us for other reasons. They funneled a big part of the money to their organization, and the rest would be spent on drugs, alcohol, clubbing, electronics, and cell phones. It is a terrible thing. The young boys have traded their tribal traditions for life similar to Tupac. It's a shame that our lifestyle in the U.S. has changed their way of thinking. They Idolize Tupac and his way of life. We feel Elvis is alive in a trailer park in south Florida, and they feel Tupac is alive and well in the swamps of Nigeria.

Just before Christmas, we went to the Dinosaur's Christmas party. They are another local motorcycle club that are good friends. All was going well for the first hour or so. Then, I sat down to eat a steak dinner and got hot and nervous. It was like an extreme anxiety attack. It is tough to explain. I have no idea what triggered it, as I was around a whole bunch of people that loved me and cared about me, so there was no reason for it. After a few minutes, Rhonda asked me what was wrong, and I told her to get me out of here now.

I stopped on the way out the door to hug my good friend Irish and apologized to him. Of course, being a Vietnam Vet, he totally understood. He hugged and kissed me, promised me things would get better, and to take care. It meant a lot to me to know that someone out there knew what I was going through.

My club Stone Cold had our Christmas Party the following Saturday, and all went well. We had a lot of fun. We passed out presents for the kids, overate, and drank a little.

In the next few days, I visited my Doctor to help with my mental stability and some antibiotics to get rid of the jungle rot. Unfortunately, I had to go through 2 rounds of antibiotics before the rot finally disappeared.

I made an appointment with a therapist and spent about an hour with him. It didn't help. I needed someone who knew how to handle what I was going through. I decided to talk with one of the guys from the ransom team and stayed in very close contact with one of the ladies from the FBI. I knew what I needed and what God had told me. I just had to figure out how to do it without pissing off my company and getting fired.

The one thing I can say is I have a strong family. From what people told me when I got back, Rhonda and Ruby were fantastic. Ruby went to school and explained to her class what had happened. It sucks that it takes something like this to bring a family closer, but that is life. But, I am happy that everyone worked so well together, there were no arrests, and no one was sent to the hospital. I still don't understand how my Mother and Grandmother got through this, but they did. I guess it is their faith in God that helped them down this jagged path.

The same goes for my Motorcycle Club; everyone worked hard to help out where they could, which also brought us closer. My brother Meatball and his wife Cindy were terrific. Rhonda could not believe how much food he had prepared in such a short time. He is one good brother, and we love him a lot.

It is hard to think about how much everyone has done for me. I feel bad not remembering who did what and where, and when.

I want to thank God, my Family, Friends, Neighbors, My club and the other clubs we are tight with, and the world for all the help and all of the prayers

## Today Show

I had many calls from the "*Today Show*," my wife and I talked to their team and talked with Matt Lauer a few times, which was great. I met with one of the men from the "*Today Show*," and we talked a little bit about what happened, then somehow got on the subject of football. He was a good man, and I told him if I interviewed with anyone, it would have to be Matt as I had a lot of respect for him.

I contacted ECO and asked for them to approve my interview. They said no. ECO would not, under any circumstances, give me the ok to do a public interview. ECO said they could stop me from doing it but would not give me their blessings. With their phrasing, I took this as you talk, you get fired. I tried everything possible to get them to let me do the interview.

I wrote my managers a second time and asked them to please ask the Chouest family again for permission to do this. About two days later, I received a text from one of the managers asking if I had heard from the family as he had passed the message and that the company's owner had asked for my phone number. Well, here it is years later, and I still haven't heard a word.

I knew talking about our experience would help me, and so did everyone else. After talking to people with the "*Today Show*," I figured out the show was going out of its way to get this done for me. But none of this was going to happen. The show finally gave up after a while. The local papers didn't feel my story was worthy enough to write about. I needed to share my story. I need to be a part of changing the rules for vessels traveling in pirate-prone waters.

I need to talk to Captains and crews about what to expect and to let them know they are not alone. For example, after our release, I learned a Marine Corps detachment was standing by right offshore from us, and I was told a Navy Seal detachment was standing by. So I kept waiting and thought that they had written us off and no one was coming to save us.

The FBI told us they had us tracked almost from the beginning and watched our every move. We knew none of this in the bush, and I knew it would have been a lot easier on us if we knew that help was nearby if critically needed.

I also wanted to set the story straight on what exactly happened. There were so many false rumors in the press that someone needed to correct them and give them the story straight from me. I was hoping at least one Senator, Congressman, U.S. Coast Guard (USCG) officer, or anyone would hear my story and say, " Hey, we need to make some changes."

There are so many agencies that could do something to change policies. But if it costs money, there's no incentive to fix it. It is easier to pay cheap insurance rates and ruin people's lives than to spend a little money, making everyone safer. And they wouldn't want downtime while making things safer.

I was told in my office during my de-briefing that I would be able to talk to the other crews and that I would be able to join in the process of making changes to policies and making the vessels more secure. Well, I am at home and haven't had a part in anything. From second hand, I found out the USCG gave the company an extension on a USCG Form 835 (Faulty Vessel/Facility Inspection Requirements) they were issued to make the boats safer. Since then, I have been taking it day by day.

# 2014

During the first week of January, I talked to HiLo, and he is ready to return to work. I am just not ready. I am frozen and snowed in, so I am just taking the time to rest. I have read a lot and watched many movies to pass the time. It's peaceful and quiet in the house. I have been passing the time helping around the house. I love to cook and have been doing a lot of that. We had a wonderful Christmas, went to Louisiana for a week, and had a great time and a Happy New Year.

One of the things my sister Brenda found in her research is that it seemed like Captain Phillip's name was one, and maybe the only name ever mentioned when a pirate attack occurred. She found that in most cases, it referred to everyone as a Captain or a chief engineer and then noted where they were from but never no names. The bottom line is no one in the world should ever have to go through what we went through. It was horrible for us and our friends and family.

It took 9/11 to force airline companies to put steel doors on the cockpits of airplanes. I wonder what it will take for someone to make the companies put bulletproof glass in the wheelhouses and stainless steel doors with hidden hinges. Or at least have a bulletproof safe room with enough room to store supplies like food, water, medications, and communication equipment. How much could it cost? You would think it would look better in the contracts to have a vessel this safe. It is especially needed on ships that carry hazardous materials. I was carrying a radioactive source on this run.

## Captain Wren Thomas' Wife, Rhonda Thomas

*Today is two months later. I am still waiting to bring my husband home. This guy I got looks like him and sometimes acts like him, but with so many things unresolved and stifled from sharing his experience. He is not yet healed. I love him dearly. I have witnessed his grief, nightmares, sleepless nights, and need for medication to cope. I have seen his anxiety and panic attacks, and anger. His inability to share his story, tell everyone what happened to him, and get the recognition he deserves has caused his grief to worsen. I am anxious for the day to come when he speaks publicly. That is the day that I will get to bring my husband home.*

## Captain Wren Thomas

Today, January 19, 2014, we went to Church. I was really happy on the way to church. I walked through the front doors and headed for the coffee bar that was always there. While standing on one side of the bar (table) fixing my coffee, I was waiting for a man to finish his on the other side so I could get some creamer packets. He was kind and asked me if I needed some cream, and I said yes, please, and he said are you sure you don't want three. He said he was a big man and always needed three. I said no two would be fine and then changed my mind and said yes, I think you were right. I do need three.

I am lucky that my church is multi-national, meaning we have members and visitors from all over the world. But, in this case, I started getting nervous. As soon as he spoke three or four words, I got nervous. I got nervous because his accent told me he was from Nigeria. If not Nigeria, then some other African country.

Knowing I have PTSD, I have been taught about triggers. It was definitely a trigger. All I wanted to do was run, I wanted out of there, and I wanted out now. I think the overwhelming feeling of wanting to hear my Pastor's message. I hate to admit it, but I am not the Christian I should be or want to be. But, I was smart enough to know that God would protect me from this Nigerian or African, and I also knew that God would carry me through the one hour of Church.

Once I went into the Chapel, I was fine. I had my Uncle Danny and my wife on one side of me, Huey and Lisa (our good friends and neighbors) on the other, with God surrounding all of us.

## CHAPTER SEVENTEEN

# Why

This same day we got home from Church. I prepared a turkey and fixed some of my special green beans for dinner. Rhonda had asked me Saturday evening if I wanted to watch the Captain Phillips movie. I had suggested waiting until tomorrow. I didn't want to watch it before I went to bed.

It was a trick I learned when I was a young child. I was okay with watching a scary movie as long as I could follow it with 6 hours of cartoons before heading to bed. The monster only got me about half the time when I did this, so the odds were in my favor of a good night's sleep.

While watching Captain Phillip's movie, I explained to my wife every time something happened in the film that happened to me. It started with the Pirates (those were my Pirates), the arguing about where the rest of his crew was on the bridge (those were my Pirates), mine argued with me on the back deck, wanting to see a crew list and wanting to find the rest of the crew; I persuaded my captors that it was in our best interest to get off the ship now, telling the pirates to take me (that was me), the ladder the pirates used (those were my Pirates),

The screaming and the guns on the ship (those were my Pirates). The screaming in the Lifeboat about who was boss, who was right, who was making the right decisions, and who wasn't (those were my Pirates). At the end of the movie, when Captain Phillips was talking to an American Navy Corpsman and couldn't speak because he was choked up and all he could do was cry (that was me).

Learning from my Mother, Step-Father, the United States Marine Corps, and being on ships for over twenty years has taught me to do what I am told. Whatever I am told to do, I do it correctly and with pride. I knew the dangers Nigeria had to offer, but I also knew that my company needed me. If I hadn't done it, someone else would have. But I'm not like that. I will not put someone else in a dangerous situation just because it is dangerous. That's not the way I roll. I compare it to other dangerous careers; Firemen, Policemen, Lawyers, Doctors, Crab Fishermen, Coalminers, etc. I did it because it was my job, and everyone told me I did it well. I took pride in my ship and company as much as I took pride in my home and family.

I have had to find help and pay for my help and medications that the insurance didn't cover. The company lied to my family. The company lied to me. Them keeping our names and faces out of the papers and off the news. That wasn't to benefit anyone other than the company. So many people who knew me didn't put two and two together.

That is why I am trying to be part of the piracy solution. We must stop piracy or get regulations that will help slow it down. To me, this is not only piracy but also terrorism. These vessels being attacked are from flagged countries other than Nigeria, Indonesia, and Somalia; in turn, it is an attack on that ship's country. It isn't a Navy ship, but it is a merchant ship. Yes, merchant mariners, we are sworn in; if needed in a time of war.

These Pirates cut through barbed wire, shoot through padlocks, and climb ladders. They are not scared to shoot out windows. They can throw grapple hooks and climb the rope, stand on a handrail and pull themselves up to the next level. And as I think it was the chief Mate on Alabama who found out, trying to fix your security devices (fire hoses) during the attack will get you killed.

In his case, I will use the word almost. Nothing you can do will 100% prevent attacks, but what it will do is it will slow down the "attack" to possibly give the Calvary time to arrive and take care of business. Also, adding another American to maintain the second watch would help if your chief officer is involved.

No matter how you maneuver the ship, these Pirates are fishermen. They are seamen, even with their small boats that spit in the face of a wake or a wave.

What I had suggested, and still feel is important, is to have a safety meeting or briefing with any Captain, chief engineer, or Office Personnel traveling to a Pirate-prone nation or sailing through or in Pirate Prone waters.

I would want to tell these men and women what to expect if they get kidnapped; I would like to explain to them that they are not alone and that someone is watching over them. I want to explain to them and give suggestions on how to handle the Pirates; for example, talking my Pirates into letting me get my meds and that having a handheld satellite phone that the pirates can steal and use for negotiations is a good thing.

I was promised I would be able to do this, and then management decided against it as it would scare people, and no one would want to go to Nigeria after this. I'm not sure what kind of shape physically the Somali Pirates were in, but again, my Nigerian Pirates were very athletic, agile, young in their 20s, and highly trained.

## CHAPTER EIGHTEEN

# Life Forever Changed

It upsets me that my company's President has not spoken a word to me to this day. He wouldn't see me when I was in the office. He hasn't called or even spent one minute sending me an email. That stabs through me like a dull knife. It is a shame. My office should feel very ashamed, but I know they don't.

Neither my managers nor Chouest Family ever called and apologized to my family. Neither my managers nor the Chouest family had called and assured my family that they would be there for them, nor accept phone calls from my sons. No one called my Mother to apologize for what happened to her son.

The two women that ECO used as pawns to come to Illinois and smooth things over are two extraordinary ladies, and I thank them for all they did to help. One of the ladies welcomed my wife into her own home and prepared a meal for her. They are both angels.

It is despicable that my ECO managers had a stranger call my wife to tell her the news of the kidnapping. It was as heartless as the kidnapping itself. Both of my managers in Louisiana have met my wife. She has sat at one of their desks more than once.

The night I was rescued, I asked my manager to call my wife to let her know I was all right but couldn't talk. He promised me he would do this, but he didn't. Again, he hid behind a third party from the negotiating team. The one thing they did was be kind enough to give my wife a $1500 advance on my salary because the FBI froze my bank accounts.

One of the things that I don't understand is why block the media. The FBI and my office say it would have been dangerous for us if the press had printed or put our names and faces in the news. How would this have been dangerous? Everyone was told that the militants would not harm us and that it was a kidnapping for ransom. The whole world already knew that it was two Americans. They could say that if everyone had a name and a face, someone would have tried to rescue us, which would have gotten us killed.

I don't believe that just because what's the difference is two Americans. What does a name and face have to do with it? No, I truly believe that between my company and the company's party negotiators that someone filled my family's head and the FBI's head full of shit.

It is one of the things that I find hard to cope with and understand. How can the world accept this kind of behavior? It would have been different if my family said no, we want privacy, and then I could understand it, but this wasn't the case. I believe our names and faces were not given to the press because this would have hurt the company. My company knew that if the world could put a story with names and faces, writers, producers, and attorneys would be knocking down our doors for the story.

I know that when I read the news or watch it on TV and hear a story, it usually doesn't impact me. But, when that story has names and faces, it significantly affects me. It does this because now I know that this is a real person. I think it is something psychological. Why was so much kept hush-hush if no one did anything wrong?

Before it was all said and done before my release, the press knew who we were, and as far as our safety in Nigeria, the Nigerians knew who we were. They had our names. We gave them our names because Seamar told us they had our documents. So I felt it safe to tell them the truth and give them our real names.

Lisa Hamby with ECO decided to ask about my mental health and wanted to offer to help pay for everything, with the condition that I release all my medical records to ECO. I wanted to end my life until I got help and put on proper meds. Every time I was alone in my house, I was trying to figure out which gun I would use and when I was driving, I was trying to figure out how I could do it in my truck. I would get so engrossed in wanting to kill myself that I would get dizzy. I hated what I put everyone through.

## It Hurts

It hurts when I don't have the answers. It hurts when I wake up, and my heart is beating wildly, terrified and sweating; what I was dreaming about, I don't know. It hurts when your mood changes more times a day than the hours on the clock.

It hurts when people around you think that the tremendous anxiety and terror that your experiencing isn't real and that it's all in your mind. It hurts knowing that the man that went into the swamps came out the other side, not a man but a monster.

It hurts when your dog seems to be the only one who always understands what you're going through. It hurts when you drink because that is the only thing that brings your mind to a stage where you can have a conversation.

It hurts when you're on your knees before bed, thanking God that you didn't commit suicide today and asking him to get you through tomorrow.

It hurts your friends and family when Pirates kidnap you once, and then your family and friends must go through the kidnapping again, "This time not by the Pirates but by Post Traumatic Stress Disorder (PTSD)."

## PTSD. It just hurts.

We can't stop piracy, but we can surely slow it down. The success of diminishing piracy on the Somalian side of Africa is proof. If companies can't or don't want to do anything about their boats being attacked, then the US Government needs to do something about it. People need to understand that this is not an act of violence. It is an act of terrorism.

A Master has to have the tools to do his job. Someone in the office creating a one hundred-page security plan does absolutely no good. With this plan, you have to have tools (cameras, a real safe room, extra radios and phones in the safe room along with food, water, and medical supplies, emergency shutdowns for the steering and main engines, pirate deterrents like sirens, instant on fire monitors, etc.).

The other thing I was promised via phone calls and emails from Chevron the day after the *C-Endeavor's* hijacking was that a security vessel would meet up with me offshore to escort me to the rig. I have never seen that security boat, but I would bet a year's salary that someone got paid for escorting us.

To this day, the only thing Chevron sends you offshore with is a shit load of supplies for the rig and a security form they make you sign. The main topic on this form is the vessel should stay at least forty-five miles from the shoreline. So tell me, what does a forty-five-mile limit do for me when the rig I am running to is ten miles off the coast?

I also agree with many people that stricter regulations are not put on these companies because we are talking oilfield, which means many bribes and kickbacks keep the regulating agencies from doing this. And the fact that Ransom Insurance is much cheaper than the cost of making ships safer.

For that ransom money, Nigerian pirates decided to change my life forever.

CHAPTER NINETEEN

# PTSD

*"I drag myself out of nightmares each morning*
*and find there's no relief in waking."*
SUZANNE COLLINS, *Mockingjay*

Things were not going well. I was seeing my doctors and thera-
pists and getting my medications changed regularly. But, I still
was not feeling right. But the hits just kept on coming.

In the spring of 2014, I was forced to archive my Masters'
License. I could not pass the DOT Physical due to the Medications I was on and the psychiatric Care. I was so proud of that
license. Now it's something else the Nigerian Pirates took from
me.

In June 2014, I was home for seven months, and things worsened. I have been back and forth with my Psychiatrist, who has
changed my meds every time I have seen him, changing around
times and doses. Everyone asks me if the meds are working. All
I can say with my entire mood swings is I think so. I haven't
committed suicide, and I am sleeping at night. I am dreaming a
lot of weird shit, but in turn, I am still getting better sleep and
getting to sleep faster.

Around June fifth I went to see my Therapist in the morning
and my Psychiatrist in the afternoon. I talked to both about

my home life and what was hurting me and disabling me from getting better. It was hard for me to deal with Rhonda thinking I hated her. I cannot stand anyone being nearby when I sleep. I also really cannot sleep at night. She is hurt thinking that I don't like her. So I decided to go home and talk with my wife and let her know that I thought it best, along with the professionals, to separate. I decided for it to work and for me to get better, it was time to pack up my horse trailer and go to Louisiana.

Once I arrived in Louisiana, I was happy, but some things took some new learning. For one, I wasn't the trusted biker I was in Illinois. So, finding a new group to spend time with and ride with was difficult. But, I finally met a few men from "Liberty Veterans M.C." I felt welcome after riding with these men and women.

My ex-in-laws were treating me like a normal person, and I am getting much-needed time with my sons and grandsons. But, it has not been easy. Since being in Louisiana, I lost a close friend in a motorcycle accident in Louisiana and a friend in Illinois.

I have been teaching my youngest son Dillon how to be a man. I have been trying to force him to take care of business on his own. He managed to buy a new truck with some of my help in co-signing, but he dealt with the car dealer and insurance on his own. Not four days later, a Nigerian-born truck driver tried to force his turn on a green light, and the truck was totaled.

## Captain Wren Thomas' Wife, Rhonda Thomas

*My husband was kidnapped twice. First, in late October 2013, he was sailing off the coast of Nigeria, just doing his job as a Ship Captain in the oilfields, and was kidnapped by Nigerian Pirates. Wow, such an unbelievable story, especially for the people in Central Illinois, where I grew up alongside my husband. I pray for exposure for this story for my husband and, selfishly, for me, too, as I still believe that bringing his story to light will help heal him from the trauma he endured.*

*My husband came home after the ordeal and was "fine." I use that word lightly, and it isn't fair to use that term, but the initial homecoming was such a relief. He was alive! It was a time to rejoice at the moment and not the time to worry about the days, weeks, and months ahead.*

*My husband has been kidnapped again. This time from our own home, by an evil bastard named PTSD.*

*When he sought counseling at the beginning for his trauma and was diagnosed with PTSD, I was so proud of him. Wow, all the things I had read about others with this evil illness had been so horrible, and my husband wasn't so horrible. Instead, he was coping very well. I was so proud that he chose to seek help when he finally opened up to me and told me about his trauma.*

*He endured so much during his first kidnapping and could talk about it. At this point, I wasn't too scared of PTSD, not on the outside anyway, not willing to tell anyone I was afraid. I sought counseling myself. I read books, blogs, and articles about PTSD. I have been consumed daily and sometimes up all night reading on my iPhone, iPad, or computer about other people and their struggles with PTSD.*

*"They" (the counselors, writers, bloggers, etc.) told me so much. They said that my husband would withdraw and start to push me away. They said that he would have good times when there were no signs of this, and then bad times when the signs would hit hard, or even sometimes hit, and we would barely notice.*

*They said to stick by him, support him, love him, and not take anything personally. That was the easy part, I didn't have to work hard to continue to love my husband, and I love him with all my heart. But, they also said that eventually, my husband would tell me that he didn't want to be with me anymore, and they said he would say his reason is that I deserve better.*

*They were so right. They said that in the end, my husband*

*would tell me that he despises me, hates me, and can't stand to look at me. That one was too hard to swallow. So I chose to park that one in my infamous proverbial back burner in my brain, the spot where I choose to park all the thoughts that I really can't deal with at the time or the ideas that are just too painful to bear. They say to continue counseling, strengthen myself, and help me understand all this.*

*I do understand, I understand all this very well, and I do not understand how more counseling to understand this will make it go away. And they say that all this will pass. I hope they are right about that.*

*Well, the truth is that I am still stinking proud of him. And proud of him for so many things; I am proud that he dared to tell his story. I can't say I would have done the same thing because I cannot imagine having that much strength. He is amazing.*

## Captain Wren Thomas

## Spiraling Out of Control

In addition to losing my Masters' License and leaving my wife, I also had to give up my Stone Cold Motorcycle Club Patch because I live out of state. So three substantial pieces of my identity as a man are lost to me because of the Nigerian pirates. I have been talking to a friend, Mohawk, who is an expert on PTSD.

We talk a lot. We have learned more about each other than we could have ever known. We talked about everything I went through and am still going through, life before and after, last night, and life this morning. Mohawk is a serious man. He doesn't pull punches, and I consider him an expert on PTSD.

He spends every minute of every day losing sleep, thinking about persons with PTSD, Veterans, and Disabled Children. He is a fighter. That two-hour phone call was more therapy than any professional has been able to accomplish; all I can say is it was wonderful, and I am so happy to have him as a coach in my corner.

He is going to help me in the fight against piracy. It is a big fight and will be a long, hard one, so now that I am fighting, I think I'll need all the people who can join my fight and stick through it to the end. I plan on going as many rounds as this fight takes.

Things have continued to spiral. I bounced between Louisiana, Illinois, Texas, and Louisiana, back home to Illinois. Without my income, Rhonda has been forced to sell our dream home. The farm we both wanted is gone, along with our horses, including my Sampson.

I have spent quite some time relating to the words in the Grand Funk Railroad song, "*I'm Your Captain*," with lyrics written by Larry Carlton. I have been to the bottom of despair, and I'm still standing. I have overdosed twice, I was so desperate for relief from the mental pain that I pulled a gun on my youngest son, Dillon, and two of his friends, hoping and begging for suicide by cop.

## Captain Wren Thomas' Sister, Brenda Wright-Rockamann

*We thought our prayers had been answered when he walked off the plane smiling and returned home to us. Wrong. Little did we know that the man who came home to us would turn into a stranger, unlike anyone we had ever met. I want to tell my story about the effect of terrorism on the family. How he may have been a prisoner for eighteen days, but then the roles reverse, and everyone he once loved or cared for suddenly becomes the hostage.*

*Hostage to his PTSD, his threats, his violent outbursts, threats of suicide, manipulation, his way or you pay. He no longer had a ship to command, so he needed to recreate what he had lost, a crew to command and control. He also needed to create the perfect lifestyle like the one he had made for himself over thirty years which had worked so effectively. In his line of work, you would be offshore for fourteen to sixty days and home for seven to thirty days, so when life would get tough at home, you would go back to work, and when work got stressful, you got to come back home.*

*An ideal setup. One that also created an excellent diversion plan for him that worked very effectively. Because he was short time everywhere he went. He had never had to be held accountable for his actions, he never once had to say he was sorry, and the only thing we had to believe was the words he told us. And why should we ever have doubted anything? That's where we got blindsided, And that's where my story begins. How terrorism not only affects the direct victim but can meticulously take down, wear down, and split a family into pieces. It is the seedy side of the story that the news never reports on; movies don't get made about it: nor do we read books about it.*

## Captain Wren Thomas

ECO cut off the extra pay they promised I would get until I could return to work (promises made to my wife and family). So I had to quit the company to get my 401K to pay off bills and get a place to live. Unfortunately, I now have no medical, dental, eye, or life insurance.

I went to see a Doctor at the Veterans Administration (VA). She added one more medication, rearranged dosages of the others, and gave me a script for two more refills, so in essence, a three-month supply of drugs that she hoped I didn't kill myself on or have even worse side effects. Then I was told I could no longer go to the VA due to the fact I was making too much money

I have applied for social security disability and supplemental social security income, as recommended by the agent for my long-term disability through The Hartford Agency.

I have applied for a service dog as per the Menninger Clinic. I sued ECO, which is a must because of the need for protection medically. Each time I have to move, I need a new psychiatrist and therapist, which means I have to start with Lisa Hamby at ECO all over again to find the necessary psychiatrist and therapist.

All of this after 28.5 years on the water. One and a half years in the USMC, and becoming a top-notch Captain for nearly 24 years, rising to a salary of almost $225,000 – $250,000 yearly.

All those 28 and a half years, I was gone from home at sea, working 2/3rds of the time and being home the other 3rd (mostly 28/14 or 60/30 Work/Home). Since graduating high school in 1984, I have never been home for more than 27 days straight, including field training in the Corps.

Until now.

There's not much I have not lost, came close to losing, or had to give up. Yet, my life has not been my life since these six words that were spoken to me on October 22, 2013, "Trust Us. Everything Will Be Okay." It only took those six words to destroy me, past, present, and future.

## CHAPTER TWENTY

# Beaux

*11 But the Lord is with me as a dread warrior; therefore
my persecutors will stumble; they will not over come
me. They will be greatly shamed, for they will not
succeed. Their eternal dishonor will never be forgotten.
12 O Lord of hosts, who tests the righteous, who sees
the heart and the mind, let me see your vengeance
upon them, for to you I have committed my cause.*
Jeremiah 20:11–12

## Beaux, PTSD Service Dog

It must have been the end of 2014 when I read the book *"Until
Tuesday."* This book is the story of a Golden Retriever Service
Dog. I loved the book and knew it would be amazing if I could
get a dog. Then, I could do things again, like go out in public.

I have virtually I shut down inside. My attorney started re-
searching service dog providers. I came across a site for "Tackett
Service Dogs" in Orange, California. While looking at their
website, I found they had Lanie, a black German Shepard, and
Beaux, a Rottweiler. I didn't study it much as I was just so excited that they were available.

I fell in love with Beaux right away. When I looked at a picture of him, I was sure those deep, melted chocolate brown eyes were looking into my soul. I wanted him. I decided the next move was to call Tackett's and get the ball rolling. I was able to talk to Tom Tackett about Beaux.

After sending him information about my kidnapping and him reading my story, he decided he would do whatever it took to match Beaux and me up. So our next step was to get sponsors to pay for Beaux, as he had a cost of $20,000.

It must have been around August 2015 when Tom called and said he wanted me to fly out to Orange to meet Beaux. It was a tough trip, as I hadn't traveled in a long time. The other difficulty to swallow was Beaux was going to like me. The way it works is just like any other dog or animal. You can love them to death, but you can't force them to like you. So I prayed to God he would love me as much as I loved him. As I said, I was more about Beaux's pictures than I was reading about him.

## Captain Wren Thomas' Sister, Sheri L. Wilson

*I was so surprised when I saw it that I had to call my brother and ask, "Tommy, did you see when Beaux was born?"*

*He said, "No, I don't notice them things."*

*I told him that he had to look. Now. I was so shocked. When he looked, I could tell when he saw it. It was as if God knew Tommy would need him. Beaux was born the same day Tommy was kidnapped.*

*Tommy agreed, "Yes, Beaux is a gift from God, and he is my gift."*

## Captain Wren Thomas

So I flew to Orange, California, to spend a week with Beaux. Tom picked us up from the airport and went to his house to meet Beaux and have some beers with his trainers. I just loved Beaux. His coat was such a beautiful, shiny black, with those deep, caramel-colored parts on his face and legs. Even his eyebrows were caramel colored. His eyes were the deep melted chocolate color I had loved in his photograph online. I still felt that this dog could see my soul. This week was supposed to be just us getting to know each other, and the second day wasn't looking good.

I asked Tom, "What do you think? Do you believe Beaux and I are a match?"

He said, "I'm not so sure. You two aren't bonding."

It was late in the afternoon, and we were at Tom's house, sitting outside. He said he had to take care of some things in town. He asked if I wanted to come or stay with Beaux. I was like, go, get out of here and leave us alone for a while.

While he was gone, I started by just petting Beaux. After a bit of petting, Beaux decided I could scratch his belly, rolling himself over with paws in the air, which is a show of trust from the animal. He slowly got used to my touch, petting and scratching him. Then Beaux allowed me to walk him around Tom's place. When Tom returned, I think he was surprised as Beaux was lying on my feet while I was sitting in a lawn chair. I think we both knew; right then, Beaux was mine.

So we spent the rest of the week with little training and bonding. The training was actually for me, not for Beaux. Beaux knew what to do, and all I knew what to do was screw things up. It was rough but fun, and I had a great time learning. The hardest thing to get over was I wasn't going to learn everything I needed to know yesterday.

I had to learn his commands, some German and some

English. But, all of this could wait for my next visit as Beaux still needed to continue learning or perfecting a few commands.

When I got out of Tom's truck at the airport, I hugged Beaux, and he couldn't stop licking my face. It surprised Tom. But Beaux and I were dudes. Two dudes that God brought together, so it didn't surprise me.

After a week of challenging fun, I flew back to Louisiana. Boy, did I miss him. I kept in contact with Tom. Tom knew I was missing Beaux, so he kept my phone busy daily with texts, pictures, and videos of and about Beaux.

I was surprised when Tom called me and told me he had obtained a sponsor to pay for Beaux. One person donated the entire $20,000.00. With that taken care of, I flew back to Orange, CA. I headed to the training field. I had the most fantastic welcome when I arrived at the training field. I hugged my new friends, and then they brought out Beaux.

Beaux ran right to me, almost knocking me over. I don't know who was more excited, him or me. He was jumping around, grabbing my hand in his mouth. It's like he was saying, "Yay! My new Daddy is here," in his own way. It was the beginning of two weeks of hard serious training. Tom and his trainers were excellent and weren't too hard on me. But I knew this was how it had to be if I wanted to qualify with Beaux.

I spent the next two weeks training and having some fun. After about the third day, Tom sat me down and told me the story of my sponsor, Miss Sally. He told me he had called her to ask her for a donation. Later in the day, she told Tom to come over and that she had a check for him to help me. He said he went and picked up the check, and when he got back in his truck, he opened the envelope to see a check for the entire $20,000. He was surprised as this never happens. Talking to her later, she told him my story compelled her. Tom asked if I wanted to meet her, and I said of course I did, so we went to lunch, and I tell you, this was rough.

We were in a fancy restaurant, and it must have been ten minutes before I could get a thank you out without bursting into tears. It was hard, as I didn't think such people existed in the world, especially good people in California. Well, I was wrong; California is full of such wonderful people. Tom qualified Beaux and me on the second anniversary of my kidnapping and on Beaux's second birthday. We made it. It was hard, and I was as nervous as a drunk in church. I knew if I wanted to bring Beaux home, I or we had to qualify to be registered as dog and handler.

My sister Sheri flew out to be there with me for our graduation. After bonding with Beaux 24 hours a day for almost two weeks, we passed. Now it was miller time. We had a benefit that night for the "Patriotic Dog Service"; this was wonderful. Again, I was walking proudly with Beaux at my side. The fundraiser was to raise funds for more people to obtain Service Dogs. It was a wonderful time as my sister and brother-in-law flew out for the event.

The following day I flew back to Louisiana with Beaux, and again I was nervous as a drunk in church as I had no idea how Beaux would act on the plane, and poor Beaux had awful gas. So it would probably be more appropriate to say, poor passengers and crew. Pee-ew.

After a successful flight back to Louisiana, I was glad to be home. I truly missed my new friends in Southern California, but like anyone else, there is no place like home. Unfortunately, I noticed Beaux had severe diarrhea during the first week at home.

I wanted to meet and greet Beaux's new doc at St. Francis Veterinary Clinic in Lafayette, Louisiana. Beaux was going in for routine shots and had severe bouts of diarrhea. Beaux was underweight, and she wanted to keep a close eye on him with his heavy diarrhea. We tried different foods, and this didn't work. Beaux wasn't getting better. He was weak and just tired all the time.

Dr. Lyons initially thought it was food allergies, as did the doctors in California. However, she said it might be stress from training and a new environment. After ruling these out, she decided it was time to do blood work. Unfortunately, it didn't come well. What should have been low was high, and what was high should have been low.

Beaux was very sick, and it was time to go further. After a series of medications and time, Beaux wasn't getting better and had lost ten pounds since being home with me. She decided to send Beaux and me to LSU Vet School in Baton Rouge, where we met Dr. Ryan. Again all I could do was pray. Dr. Ryan immediately scheduled a biopsy on Beaux's intestinal tract. I was scared this was a $2,000 plus procedure. My prayers were answered, and Dr. Ryan's team paid for the procedure, which was good news but resulted in bad news.

My baby Beaux had inherited "Helicobacter," "Inflammatory Bowel Disease," and "Lymphangiectasia." All killer diseases. Dr. Ryan couldn't believe what he found as these are not found in Rottweilers and are more common in smaller dogs. Dr. Ryan ended up calling Germany to find out they had cases of these diseases in Rottweiler's. All we could do was use heavy medications and a very strict diet. About a week later, I noticed a change in Beaux's stool, and he started gaining weight. Everyone at St. Francis was so excited, including me.

Beaux's energy went through the roof. After about a month, I got a call from Dr. Lyons, and she told me, Wren, this is a miracle. She could not believe how fast Beaux was responding. Beaux is doing great and finally started gaining weight, and I don't think he will stop gaining. Beaux is a solid boy.

## Captain Wren Thomas' Sister, Kari Tiffey

*When Tommy found out he was getting Beaux, it gave him hope. It was actually the first time we had seen our brother's big smile that he used to always have before the kidnapping!*

## Captain Wren Thomas

In January 2016, I got an email from the Doctors wanting to know if it was ok if they elected Beaux as "Pet of the Year" for 2015 for the state of Louisiana. I cried a yes in an email back. It was the last weekend of January when I took Beaux to Shreveport to receive the awards. I knew I had to say a few words, but when I was called up to the podium, all I could get out was a thank you through all the tears. I was so excited about all the miracles with Beaux that all I could do was cry.

Beaux has blown away his Vets with how his health is so remarkable as this is a killer disease. Beaux and I spend every second of every day with each other. We wake up, and Beaux will eat while I drink my morning coffee. After Beaux has eaten, he feels it's time to become my lapdog and jumps up in my lap, all 85 pounds of him.

After this love time, we go outside so he can play chase the tennis ball. He is a nut. He refuses to go potty if I don't throw the ball first, and then and only then does he go, kind of like an older man with a newspaper.

I cannot work anymore, so it usually ends up being days of him exercising with his ball. Then we make our rounds at the gym, family, and whatever shopping needs to be done, we come home for some training and play. But, of course, play means more chasing the tennis ball.

Beaux has become very fond of my granddaughter, Olivia (Dillon's daughter). She is a year and a half and scatters food everywhere, so as you can imagine, he follows her around. They are partners in crime.

With Beaux, I feel safer. I am no longer a hermit. I go out, knowing that Beaux is there. Beaux will "Block" when I sit down, or if I want him to be between me and someone else when we are out and about, I will tell him, "Cover," and he will stand on my right side facing behind me to watch my back from the monsters.

When I experience a panic attack in public, Beaux will either jump up on me or push all his weight against me. When he does this, I usually kneel and pet him and love on him, trying to get my head straight again.

With the reassurance that Beaux would have my back and help me through the panic, I started feeling more like me. This includes talking to my wife, Rhonda. While we were separated and had begun to divorce, we realized that's not what either of us truly wanted. So Beaux and I moved back home to Illinois.

I have my own place. In my space, I have a sense of peace and safety. In my home, I have Beaux. I was able to start dating my wife, Rhonda, again. Rhonda visits or eats dinner, and we work on our relationship. It's nice. I never didn't love her. But, I simply couldn't be with her. I couldn't sleep in a bed with anyone. I couldn't stand the thoughts of the changes in me not being the man she married. But in 2017, Rhonda and I officially got back together. We live in the same town, just in separate homes. Rhonda and Ruby have a house, and I have a house.

After Rhonda leaves, Beaux and I will come in and rest and watch some TV. Then it is time for bed. Sleeping is still rough for me. I have many nightmares. Beaux is pretty good about waking me up during these nightmares. He chews on my hand, lays on me with all his weight, or nudges me with his nose. When my nightmares are more violent, all Beaux can do is get off the bed. I usually wake up when I hear his feet hit the hardwood floor.

I'm not sure how I would sleep without Beaux. I can't really sleep at night due to concerns of someone coming and attacking me, so I sleep in bits, some during the day and some in the early evening while the sun is still up. I cannot sleep with others in the house. I cannot trust my violent nightmares and would never forgive myself if I were to hit Rhonda, one of the kids, or my grandchildren. Thank goodness Beaux can adjust to my very messed up sleeping schedule.

I have to say Beaux is doing well, and I think with prayers and good Doctors, Beaux will live beyond expectations. I cannot imagine moving forward without Beaux. We are an inseparable pair.

Having Beaux with me has allowed me to have a life again. However, I still cannot live with my wife. I do not want to hurt her in my sleep. I couldn't live with myself if I accidentally hurt her. PTSD is something that I have learned to deal with, but it will likely never completely go away. Here it is, 2019, six years later, and I still have so many violent nightmares and dreams.

## Captain Wren Thomas' Sister, Kari Tiffey

*Beaux saved Tommy's soul. He was in a very dark place. Suicidal, mixing prescription drugs with alcohol, anything that would numb the mental pain. Beaux needed him as much as he needed Beaux. There is something in the numbers we have always believed. Beaux was born on the day Tommy was kidnapped.*

*For two years, while Beaux was being groomed and trained for his human, Tommy was fighting to stay alive mentally. The grin on our brother's face was a glimmer of our old brother, the one we once knew.*

## Captain Wren Thomas

Lately, Beaux has been tired. He's slowing down. I'm unsure if it is aging or something else bothering him. But Rhonda and I agreed that Beaux is not himself, so I plan to take him to the veterinarian's office and have him checked out.

After visiting the vet and speaking with him about Beaux, we agreed to try some things at home to help Beaux feel better. Beaux has always had the spirit of a fighter and survivor. He has overcome so much.

More vet visits and Beaux has become more and more lethargic. Each time the vet comes up with a new suggestion to help Beaux get back to normal. So we go home and try, but Beaux continues to be increasingly sedentary no matter what we do.

Today the vet told me it was time to let him go. So Beaux was put to sleep. Unfortunately, after his death, the vet discovered cancer throughout Beaux.

I don't know how I will be without my best dude here with me, but I would never want him to suffer just to stay with me.

CHAPTER TWENTY-ONE

# Need for Increased Safety Measures

*When life seems hard, the courageous do not lie
down and accept defeat, they are all the more
determined to struggle for a better future.*
Queen Elizabeth II

In 2013, twenty-five governments in the Western African Gulf area met in Cameroon to sign the Yaoundé Code of Conduct. This agreement created a new maritime security concept, with a heavy focus on information and intelligence sharing. The Yaounde Code of Conduct also has elements to coordinate naval operations. The goal is to identify and apprehend criminal or terrorist groups to protect seafarers and deter would-be pirates. In addition, five West African countries established multinational maritime coordination centers. The remaining nineteen countries bordering the gulf have also set up operational bureaus.

Nigeria passed piracy-suppression laws in 2019, which promise the prosecution of arrested pirates and other criminals. However, it took until August 2020 for a Nigerian court to sentence the first three pirates under this law after they hijacked an Equatorial Guinean cargo ship.

Over forty percent (40%) of piracy incidents that occurred in 2020 took place in West African waters. In addition, 95% of all kidnapped crew members were taken from ships transiting the Gulf of Guinea.[5]

Efforts are underway to fight against piracy, oil theft, smuggling, and illegal fishing. Many of these efforts participate in the Integrated National Security and Waterways Protection Infrastructure project, known as Deep Blue. Deep Blue funding has provided coastal patrol vehicles, interceptor boats, and reconnaissance aircraft to work together for vessel protection.

In July 2021, Nigerian President Muhammadu Buhari commissioned a surveillance system to provide a comprehensive picture of Nigeria's maritime environment. In addition, he deployed troops on land in Nigeria to assist in apprehending criminal or terrorist groups and their assets.

The efforts of Deep Blue have been credited for the decline in piracy in the Gulf of Guinea in 2021[6]. Of course, we must also credit the regional governments, the shipping industry, and foreign navies. But, of course, better policing at sea doesn't address challenges on land that help drive locals to piracy.

European Union (EU) countries and the United States have increasingly deployed naval vessels to the Gulf of Guinea to combat organized criminal groups targeting commercial transport ships. For example, the Danish navy sent a frigate to the Gulf of Guinea in November 2021. Additional countries, such as France, Spain, Portugal, and the US, have their navies routinely patrol West African waters. In addition, the US hosts multinational naval exercises in the Gulf of Guinea that improve counter-piracy operations and impede illegal fishing.

In June 2022, the United Nations (UN) issued a resolution that condemned piracy in the Gulf of Guinea, considered the world's most dangerous piracy hot spot[7].

---

[5] https://www.washingtonpost.com/politics/2022/06/09/gulf-of-guinea-piracy/
[6] https://nimasa.gov.ng/international-maritime-bureau-confirms-piracy-decline-in-the-gulf-of-guinea/
[7] https://press.un.org/en/2022/sc14915.doc.htm

The ICC International Maritime Bureau Piracy and Armed Robbery Against Ships report ending March 31, 2022, states, "... all waters in/off Nigeria remain highly risky. Vessels are advised to be vigilant as many incidents may have gone unreported. Kidnapping for ransom remains the biggest risk for crews. Therefore, it is recommended that vessels take additional measures in these high-risk waters[8]."

There are broader challenges across West Africa, especially in the Niger Delta. For example, tackling corruption, poverty, and environmental degradation remains essential for reducing the demand for maritime piracy and other types of sea crimes. But addressing these broader challenges, experts point out, will also require assistance from the international community.

I am still driven to educate Captains, Masters, and all merchant mariners about piracy. There is so much this industry can do to protect the personnel. I have a good deal of information to share with the mariners to ensure they survive if their ships are hijacked and taken hostage.

## Captain Wren Thomas' Mother, Judy Davis-King

*Talk about the word Courage. They say that courage is "having the ability to conquer fear or despair"; he had both.*

*A Hero is one that is much admired or shows great courage; he had both.*

*He is a son, husband, father, brother, uncle, cousin, nephew, grandfather, grandson, and a good friend to all.*

*He is our hero.*

*I love you, son.*

---

8   https://www.icc-ccs.org/reports/Q1%202022%20IMB%20Piracy%20Report.pdf

## Captain Wren Thomas

At present, life has been rough since returning from Nigeria. It has been very hard on us as I went to Nigeria as one man and returned as another. I was diagnosed formally with severe Post Traumatic Stress Disorder and have been on Social Security Disability since 2017. I hope to return to normal soon with a lot of help, medication, church, therapy, and relaxation time. However, I realized that my new normal is never going to be as I knew it before the Nigerian Pirates decided the need to change my life forever.

All of this is summed up in 6 words:
*"Trust us. Everything will be okay."*

THE END